FIRE OVER ENGLAND

A British Picture

FIRE OVER ENGLAND

The British Cinema Comes Under Friendly Fire

Ken Russell

HUTCHINSON

© Ken Russell 1993
Photographs © The Kobal Collection 1993

The right of Ken Russell to be identified as Author of this work has been asserted by Ken Russell in accordance with the Copyright, Designs and Patents Act 1988

9 8 7 6 5 4 3 2 1

This edition first published in 1993 by
Hutchinson
Random House (UK) Limited
20 Vauxhall Bridge Road, London, SW1V 2SA

Random House Australia (Pty) Ltd
20 Alfred Street, Milsons Point, Sydney, NSW 2061,
Australia

Random House New Zealand Ltd
18 Poland Road, Glenfield, Auckland 10,
New Zealand

Random House South Africa (Pty) Ltd
PO Box 337, Bergvlei 2012, South Africa

A CIP catalogue record for this book is available from the British Library

Typeset by Deltatype Ltd, Ellesmere Port
Printed and bound in Great Britain by
Clays Ltd, St Ives plc

ISBN 0 09 174569 1

1000173648

To Mum

We all see films differently. Memory also has a tendency to re-edit, re-shoot even re-dub. A line like 'Play it again, Sam', even when the original dialogue is known to be different, identifies *Casablanca* immediately. So if you should find within these pages any descriptions that conflict with the facts, they are that way, because that's how I remember them.

Ken Russell

Contents

I

Fires Were Started

My mouth was on fire. I gulped down one glass of iced water and then another. 'How about calling it *Fire Over England*?' suggested my publisher, with a smile. I laughed, nodded — anything was better than something like *Ken Russell's View of the British Film from Childhood to the Present Day*.

We were kicking around ideas for a book on this subject over lunch in an Indian restaurant and, as a result of my reckless assault on a vicious Chicken Vindaloo, up popped a title. At first I was inclined to dismiss it but as my digestive juices got to work I realised with a burp that it really had something going for it. After all, didn't the British film come of age in the last war when many of our cinemas were going up in flames?

As a child I remember cycling down the smouldering ruins of Southampton High Street the morning after our worst Blitz. Gone were most of the old familiar landmarks. Gone was the Cadena Café where a ladies' string trio had played 'Tea for Two' as Mum and I took some light refreshment after a matinée at the Picture House. Gone was the Picture House!

A tear crept into my eye as the realisation came that I would probably never see my favourite fairy cakes again. I would probably never see 'Old Mother Riley' again, either. I cheered up instantly. Every dark cloud has a silver lining. I hated Old Mother Riley and her monopoly of the Picture House, and glowed at the thought of never having to see him again — yes, him, because Old Mother Riley was actually Arthur Lucan in drag. His wife, Molly, played her daughter – all very incestuous and terribly boring; a dreary music hall act about an Irish washerwoman and her unattractive offspring transferred to the screen with minimum cost and imagination. Drab, dull and dreadful; even Mum who was an avid film fan found them boring.

The only reason Mum patronised the Picture House was because the second half of the double bill, which was usually an American movie, often featured a favourite of hers – Gene Autry, the singing cowboy. Frankly I wasn't mad about him, either – he shot his mouth off more than he shot his guns.

Luckily the cinema opposite the demolished Picture House had survived. That was the Odeon, where I had enjoyed many a Busby Berkeley musical and endured endless Wurlitzer organ intermissions, often including an exotic piece of kitsch by Albert Ketèlbey of 'In a Persian Market' fame.

Further down the High Street, I was surprised to see the old Gaiety was still standing. The most memorable thing I saw there was Mum's face the night she lost a ten-shilling note and made me swear – cross my heart and hope to die – never to tell Dad. Ten bob was a small fortune in those days. The Gaiety was the home of American B movies, often featuring John Carradine as a starving beachcomber. I rather wished they'd got the Gaiety too.

The Empire, down by the flattened docks, where I had encountered my first child molester, was also miraculously still standing. Apart from that weird sexual encounter in the dark, when Pinocchio's nose had grown in direct proportion to my willie, I had enjoyed my visits to the Empire and *Hellzapoppin* most of all. But as I pedalled around Southampton, visiting all those old familiar places – the Atherley, the Rialto, the Palladium, the Broadway, the Forum – I was increasingly gratified to see that out of Southampton's twenty-seven cinemas there had been only two fatalities.

Amid the mountains of bricks and twisted metal, the twenty-five survivors rose up defiantly as monuments to whatever it was that made life worthwhile to a goodly proportion of the population. True, most of the churches had also survived. But, for the most part, they were monuments to boredom. It was never standing room only in there. No, it wasn't the church that kept Mum going during the pre-war years, or even through the war itself, for that matter. If anything sustained her and thousands like her, it was not the example of saints and angels from the Holy Bible, but their Hollywood counterparts. Not Saints Peter and Paul but Peter Lorre and Paul Muni. I think Mum would have gone mad without the movies.

Uneducated and a victim of a loveless marriage, with a maid to do all the housework and plenty of time to kill every afternoon, Mum would have been like a lost soul without the congregations of kindred spirits sitting side by side in the dark. Sitting beside her, with a choc-ice, I must confess that more often than not I felt like the odd man out. I would have been just as happy playing in the garden, indulging in my own fantasies rather than sharing other people's. If it was a Western epic or a swashbuckling costume drama, then I would happily surrender; but soppy love stories with big black-and-white close-ups of slobbering lips left me cold.

I had no choice. Mum always wanted me along for company as a sort of chaperon. Even as late as the Thirties, it was not the done thing for a woman to visit the cinema unaccompanied – even for a matinée. But the toy six-guns I occasionally toted were no deterrent for some of the big bad wolves prowling in the dark, and many was the time we were forced to leave without getting our money's worth.

Mum usually saved the best picture of the week for Dad, who accompanied her every Wednesday evening – out of duty rather than pleasure. That's how I came to miss *Things to Come* and *The Old Dark House*. So it wasn't long before I started taking the law into my own hands, and, with the aid of *Picturegoer* which reviewed all the new releases, began choosing my own programmes. Several times a week, after school, I'd pay my threepence and have a good wallow.

Penny by penny, I graduated from Shirley Temple to Betty Grable. By the time I was sent away to the Nautical College, Pangbourne at the age of thirteen, I was so hopelessly smitten by the Hollywood sex goddesses that I would risk corporal punishment to worship at their shrines in nearby Reading, which was strictly out of bounds. I generally liked my stars in exotic roles, preferring Betty Grable in *Song of the Islands* to *April Showers*, although I did enjoy the see-through plastic mac in the 'Run Little Raindrop Run' number. I adored Hedy Lamarr as Tondelayo – the dusky native girl who drives the white man mad with desire in *White Cargo*. Dorothy Lamour got me pretty hot under the collar, too, especially when strutting her stuff in a sarong in *Aloma of the South Seas*. Between them, these lily-white ladies covered from head to foot in brown body make-up kindled in me a desire to sail away to the tropics and 'go native'. All I had to do was complete my training as a naval cadet and apply for a berth on a ship going south. In the meantime I would fulfil my other ambition – to see as many films as possible.

I could not get enough of them and, although I suffered great deprivation in term time, I more than made up for it in the hols with the aid of my BSA sports bike and a number of first, second and third run cinemas. By pedalling daily from one end of Southampton to the other, with occasional trips on the floating bridge, I managed to view around fifty films in the spring and winter holidays, and about seventy-five in the summer season. This often entailed cycling further afield to outlying districts such as Totton and Eastleigh, and sometimes even further. I well remember sweating up Pepper Box Hill one hot summer's day on my way to Salisbury to see Bambi's mother die in a blizzard of Technicolor snow.

During term time I was able to do a little catching up, without playing truant, since every other week we had a film show in the College gymnasium. After singing dirty sea-shanties outside in the dark, we were made to fall in and march inside for a basinful of British comedy, often featuring Will Hay, a prune-faced, short-sighted, crumpled, middle-aged man in pince-nez, who frequently wore a mortar board and wielded a cane, as in *Boys Will Be Boys*. It seemed that we couldn't get away from the classroom, even on Saturday night.

One of his better efforts was *My Learned Friend*, about a murderer on the rampage, bent on bumping off everyone responsible for putting him behind bars, including his fatuous defence lawyer played, of course, by Will Hay. The funniest sequence involves a mix-up in a lunatic asylum, with our hero on all fours pretending to be a dog, in order to humour someone he imagines to be a dangerous maniac. In reality it's the chief psychiatrist who naturally thinks the yapping Will is completely insane.

The climax comes in the Houses of Parliament with Will Hay dressed as a Beefeater, swinging with the killer on the hands of Big Ben. Maybe you remember a similar sequence in the remake of the remake of *The 39 Steps*. Only this time Robert Powell was involved and it wasn't meant to be funny.

Old Bones of the River wasn't very funny either, though I suppose it was meant to be. It was set in darkest Africa where, according to a sub-title 'a handful of Englishmen rule half a million natives – teaching the black man to play the white man, and play up and play the game'. It was very racist, even to the extent of having one black man say to another black man, 'Stop acting like a dirty nigger.' Will Hay was Deputy District Commissioner as far as I can remember, and dispensed justice and wisdom to the natives thus:

ZULU: May I have another wife, Master? The nights are long.
WILL HAY: Get up earlier.

Several cadets eventually became Colonial Administrators themselves, and I sometimes wonder if they modelled themselves on
Will Hay. He specialised in figures of authority who were both
ineffectual and bogus, but eventually triumphed through their
very ineptitude. In many ways, he became a role model for civil
servants for generations to come.

He once played a hapless station master in *Oh Mr Porter*, in the
days when our railways ran on time and, although he is dead and
gone, his ghost still haunts British Rail. Of course, the porter has
now become a thing of the past. I discovered this the other day on
my return to England after a few months' stay in America. Laden
with luggage I foolishly hailed the first British Rail man that caught
my eye. 'Porter!' I shouted across the busy station concourse.

All of Euston fell silent. Jaws dropped and eyes gaped. The
'porter' didn't blink an eyelid, but turned his back in contempt and
slowly walked away. Later, after I had lugged all my cases on to the
train, a kindly old guard pointed out my social gaffe. 'Porter' was a
dirty word now – both insulting and degrading, like 'tits' or
'nigger'. The title I should have used was 'Station Attendant'.

Unlike most little Hitlers, Will Hay allowed himself to be
upstaged by his inferiors, especially by Graham Moffatt, a cheeky
fat boy, and Moore Marriott, a crotchety old gent with a beard.
Maybe that's what made him endearing, despite his dictatorial
attitude. One thing that never struck me as odd at the time is that
there were never any women in his films – other than in bit parts.
He moved exclusively in a world of men. Maybe he was afraid of
women, like most of his fans at our sex-starved Nautical College . . .

In this regard, he was the antithesis of another College favourite,
the lanky, lantern-jawed Jack Hulbert. He usually played the
underdog who got the better of his betters. In *Jack Ahoy*, he was an
able-bodied seaman who ended up with the Admiral's daughter,
with a song and a dance on the way. 'She's got me walking on the
tip of my toes, and the hat's on the side of my head.' True, he was

no Gene Kelly, but he does a wonderful rubbery hornpipe here that is almost cartoon-like in character. He'd have made a perfect partner for Betty Boop-a-doop-doop. Instead, he saves the Admiral's daughter from a gang of Chinese pirates. Our college magazine advertised it as 'Hi jinx among the Chinks'. Once again, a true Brit teaches the revolting natives a lesson in manners and defeats an army of chattering orientals single-handed. Whenever I see a Spielberg action adventure movie, I am struck by a curious similarity to those jingoistic novelties.

Many of the films we saw at College either glorified Great Britain or had something to do with the sea. *Contraband*, with Conrad Veidt as the handsome captain of a Danish merchantman, was typical. It was a light, romantic comedy with bondage overtones.

The captain, confronted by two heavies at gunpoint, is asked to reveal his identity.

'I am Andersen,' he says, 'Hans Andersen.'

'And we are the Brothers Grimm,' reply the heavies.

There's a memorable scene when the captain is tied up back to back with the heroine in two chairs.

'I shall hurt you,' he says, as he prepares to struggle free.

'Go ahead,' she says.

She grimaces in agony as he twists and turns to loosen his bonds. Then, free at last, he kisses her on the lips while she remains bound hand and foot. All strangely provocative.

I think that was the kinkiest film we ever had at the Nautical College, which would have made a good film in itself. Most of the films on public schools I've come across never quite capture the spirit of the real thing. *Tom Brown's Schooldays* was the first and, although it was set in 1854, things were not all that different at my school in 1944. Not only was there bullying and corporal punishment at the Nautical College, but also masturbating in chapel and even worse down at Bartholomew's Bottom – a secluded dell in the Cadets' Wood. However, the film did have one dubious character,

7

called Flashman, who got up to no good at the local farm. Whether he was screwing the dairymaids or the sheep was left entirely to the imagination.

Lindsay Anderson's *If* . . . brilliantly captures the sadistic side of the public school system. New boys are called 'Scum', and treated like slaves by the seniors, who never miss a chance to humiliate them – either by caning them on the bottom or getting them to warm the lavatory seat – 'I shall be along in five minutes.' There is a great deal of anal fixation – and fantasy too. Malcolm McDowell in a café, flirting with a girl behind the counter, imagines they are rolling around naked on the floor. But dreams turn to reality when he leads a full-scale revolt on Founders' Day, machine-gunning the whole bloody establishment as they troop out of chapel – the parents, the masters and their collaborators, the seniors – the whole rotten lot. Who, at one time or another, has not wanted to bayonet the boring padre, especially if he's a captain in the officers' training corps? But fantasy has its rules, and you break them at your peril. By resurrecting the padre in the office of the head-master, and making him exact an apology from the offenders for killing him, Anderson is guilty of cheating. It profoundly diminishes the impact of his message. For it seems to me that *If* . . . – which attacks all the bullshit Kipling's famous poem celebrates –is a metaphorical movie about mixed-up Merrie England, which shows how her poets, philosophers and free spirits are brutalised by a repressive establishment and its attendant toadies.

I have very mixed feelings about my public school – the Nautical College, Pangbourne. It's still going strong and even has its own film group. I wonder if they've still got a copy of the first film I ever made there? It was called *The Maiden and the Monster* – a social satire on the infamous College sausage, which would have served better as a policeman's truncheon.

After a horrendous start, I had a good time at Pangbourne, but I'm not sure if they were the happiest days of my life. If there had been a mix-up at the Ministry of Education and a girls' school had suddenly been billeted on us they might well have been.

That supposition was the basis of *The Happiest Days of Your Life*, directed by Frank Launder. The way the two heads put their heads together in an effort to dampen their pupils' ardour was classic. Margaret Rutherford was at her eccentric best as the pompous Mrs Whitchurch and Alastair Sim excelled as the long-suffering headmaster. He later went on, in *The Belles of St Trinian's*, to play the headmistress!

My happiest day as a scholar was my last, when I put on the first drag show the College had ever seen. It was largely a homage to Hollywood, and featured such stars as Dorothy Lamour and Betty Grable. I made a passable Dottie in those days (with the help of a couple of rugger socks tucked up my sarong) and my best friend was Betty Grable's double. No British stars, you notice. I wonder why? Maybe they just didn't count. Who were they, anyway?

There was always Gracie Fields of *Shipyard Sally* fame.

'Sally, Sally, pride of our alley, you're more than the whole world to me.'

She had a voice like a fog horn, sang about dogs pissing on aspidistras, was as plain as Lancashire hotpot and had an accent to match. Hardly an image to kindle a young cadet's ardour.

Then there was Jessie Matthews who was stuck up and spoke as if she had a plum in her mouth. Who else? Oh yes, Anna Neagle – before she moved up the social scale to make those awful musicals like *Maytime in Mayfair*. She was quite something in *Nell Gwyn*, an early effort directed by Herbert Wilcox. It was quite racy for its day, and had boundless energy and style. Anna Neagle was really quite cute with her saucy smile and boyish curly blonde hair.

'I know what you want,' she says, winking to an admirer and pulling up her skirt. 'The price of a drink.'

Whereupon she produces a coin from the purse attached to her garter. She is also kindly and considerate, as when someone calls her rival a shameless foreign whore,

'You must be fair to her,' responds Nell, 'she can't help being foreign.'

And she can dance, whether in short pants and silk hose or long court dresses. And although she mugs like mad she has bags of vitality. For once, there is no pretence that Nell was anything but a trollop in pursuit of the Monarch she eventually seduces in the aptly named King's Arms. Fade out.

Fade in next morning with Nell in a double bed, hugging a pillow, twiddling her thumbs and looking well pleased with herself, as the satisfied King slowly gets dressed. Somehow, it was far more erotic than anything Margaret Lockwood ever did in her many roles as the 'wicked lady'. I suppose she was another contender in the sex appeal stakes, although I never saw her in a swimsuit. Come to think of it, I never saw any of these women in a swimsuit and I never saw them in Technicolor either, at least up until 1945. They were simply not pin-up material. They had no GLAMOUR and were as dull as the films in which they starred.

For my tenth birthday, my parents had given me a Pathescope Ace hand-cranked home movie projector and a silver screen. From that moment, my film education began. My subjects included comedy, drama, acting, editing, lighting, make-up, design and composition. I learned my lessons by running a handful of films over and over again, until I knew every scene, every cut, every frame. I started with thirty- and sixty-foot extracts which came in tin canisters you clipped on to the projector. The film stock was 9.5 mm wide and had a sprocket hole at the top-centre of each frame. Because the picture was almost the same area as professional 16 mm film (which has sprocket holes down the side) the quality of the image was pin sharp.

But what of the films themselves? To start with they all came from the silent era, some might say the Golden Era. When I first saw them, over fifty years ago as a boy in Southampton, they were already museum pieces. Nevertheless, these movies changed my life and became a yardstick against which I have measured most movies ever since. Later I added directors like Cocteau, René Clair, Vigo and Welles to my list, but the two artists who inspired me then were Charlie Chaplin and Fritz Lang. Old Mother Riley was very drab in comparison.

Those two-minute snippets from *The Rink* and *The Cure* left me hungry for more. The Pathescope catalogue advertised complete versions on three hundred-foot reels, but they were too expensive to buy and anyway my projector wasn't designed to take eight-inch spools. However, the films could also be hired from a chemist's shop around the corner, and I had another birthday coming up.

The extension arms I received as a present transported me even further into the realms of wonder. Chaplin's films were a continuing source of enjoyment, but the fantastic world of Fritz Lang appealed to me even more. Dragons, dwarfs, invisible men and ravishing princesses rubbed shoulders with mad scientists, magnificent heroes, glamorous robots, dream forests, hallucinations, omens, symbols and cities of the future.

The fact that the Germans were bombing the hell out of us as we watched didn't mean a thing to me. I realised at an early age that art has no frontiers. The proceeds of these shows, given in Dad's garage to the neighbours, went to our local Spitfire Fund, so in no way did I feel like a saboteur. As Siegfried slew the fire-breathing dragon and the incendiaries rained down, I had a hero of my own to fight the flames, for Dad was a member of the Auxiliary Fire Service. So I also used to give shows to the crew at the local fire station whenever possible.

As you'd expect, the Chaplin comedies always went down well, but, to my surprise, the men preferred *Siegfried* and his epic battle with the dragon. If you are unfamiliar with this silent classic, imagine a rocky ravine and a fur-clad warrior slashing away at that medieval flame-thrower as it tries to scorch the furry pants off him. When the roars of laughter subsided, the air raid sirens' awful wail coincided neatly with the dragon's agonised demise as it got one in the eye from Siegfried's magic sword.

Moments later the place was empty, and I was on the way down Winchester Road on a fire engine heading for the J. Arthur Rank flour mills that were already in flames. At Number 309, the appliance pulled up. I jumped out and ran to the garden shelter, where my younger brother, Ray, was sleeping in a bunk and Mum was sipping tea from a thermos. I barely had time to sit down before the sound of an express train whistling like a banshee split the air. An explosion rocked the shelter. Two more express trains rushed through the air and blew themselves apart – nearer and nearer! The next one, the loudest of all, seemed as though it was about to come straight through the roof. I bit my lip, covered my ears ... and waited an eternity. But this time there was no explosion – just the receding drone of a Dornier III at 10,000 feet.

Ray was still sleeping but Mum said, 'Go and have a look, Ken.' Shakily I went up the steps. The smell of explosives was heavy in the air. Suddenly I felt an intense stinging pain in my left eye. I yelled out.

'What's up, Ken?' Mum shouted.

For a moment I couldn't answer, eyes tight shut and tears pouring down my face.

Mum repeated the question, more urgently.

I remained speechless. 'I'm blind,' I thought. 'I shall never see Siegfried again!' Then I managed to pull myself together sufficiently to stammer, 'I walked straight into the rose bush, Mum. I think I've got a thorn in my eye.'

'Come indoors and we'll have a look at it,' she said. 'Must have been a dud.'

Later we discovered there was an unexploded bomb outside the front door. It didn't go off and I didn't go blind either. I lived to see Siegfried metamorphose into Hopalong Cassidy. Yes, the blond Aryan survived to star in many a B movie Western – always dressed in black. If his Hopalong films were bland, they were not necessarily boring, unlike the films made about the AFS – *The Bells Go Down* and *Fires Were Started*. They were more like documentaries than feature films. They had to be. They were not about individuals but stereotypes. The fact that these films featured real firemen counts for nothing when the dialogue is so banal and stilted.

We had to wait for *Hope and Glory* for a film on the Blitz that is free of propaganda and phoney heroics. What's more, it is a personal view – the view of an imaginative film-maker who was there. After all the films we were obliged to endure in the war featuring stiff upper lips, this was soft and slobbery.

I vividly remember our school of 760 pupils boarding the train at Southampton Central in a quiet and orderly manner. There was a holiday mood in the air because we were all off to the seaside. In the capital, it was a far different story – as far as John Boorman remembers it through the eyes of nine-year-old Bill. In *Hope and Glory* chaos and hysteria reign and Bill's mum does her nut. Most of the mums in Southampton were glad to see the back of us for a while. But Bill's mum, crying and screaming, leaps the barrier and drags her wee ones back to the bosom of the family home, which is promptly blown apart.

John's wartime school seemed a lot less pleasant than mine, with the headmaster caning a boy while praying for victory. I didn't much care for his geography teacher either, pointing at a map of the world and shrilling, 'Two fifths of the pink bits are ours. Our men are fighting and dying to save all the pink bits for you.' To me that sort of attitude sounds like someone being wise fifty years after the event. However, maybe it's not just poetic licence, maybe it really was all like that. It's his story, not mine.

To the younger generation, bored with black-and-white re-runs of the war as seen on TV, *Hope and Glory* must be a real Technicolor eye-opener on everything they missed – G I Joes, black-market nylons, shrapnel, ration books, incendiary bombs, barrage balloons, digging for victory and the death of the mother of the little girl next door. John's film also shows the terrible beauty of war, as when a teenager sees her home disintegrating into a million pieces in one stupendous blast of light.

Boorman started his career making documentaries for the BBC. So did John Schlesinger, who also made a Technicolor extravaganza about the last war many years after the event. It is called *Yanks*, and chronicles the impact of the US Army on a small town in Yorkshire. Apart from the perennial topic of the weather, the emphasis is on sex and social taboos, like 'No nigger gonna jive with a white woman less he wants his teeth pushed down his throat and a swift kick in the balls.' The protracted sequence showing race hatred erupting in a dance hall is the highlight of the film, illustrating for the first time on the screen the darker side of the US occupation. Such acts were fairly commonplace, I gather. I've also heard rumours of a lynching or two, though of course this sort of thing was kept heavily under wraps at the time. So was the high rate of homosexuality in the US forces. When I saw Richard Gere failing to make it in bed with a lovely English rose, I thought Schlesinger was about to tackle that forbidden subject as well. It had been hinted at all along, for gentle, doe-eyed Richard plays a fastidious army chef who keeps his kitchen spotless, and is a dab hand at making fruitcakes with pretty pink icing. But we are fobbed off with a limp excuse about commitment and so on.

Maybe Schlesinger's nerve failed him at the last moment. There's not a limp wrist in sight nor a single hard on in the shower room. The entire male cast is heterosexual to a man, yet, according to some statistics, one GI in ten on active service was gay. All we get is a series of conventional love affairs. It would have been so much more exciting to see Richard Gere larking about on the moors with a member of the Home Guard.

Part of the fun of the film is trying to guess in which reel the various women involved will surrender to that irresistible New World charm. 'Let me through, I'm pregnant,' shouts one expectant mother, elbowing her way through the crowd of sobbing women on the station platform, in the last sequence of the film. 'So's half the bloody town,' shouts another.

The film ends with tearful goodbyes and train smoke. Not a word about the epidemic of syphilis the boys left behind, before their major sexual assault on the Continent.

II

Carry on at Sea

Before the war was over I, too, waved goodbye to my loved ones (Mum, Dad and brother Ray) and caught a train – to Liverpool. The one and only film I saw there was called *Laura*, and featured Gene Tierney, Clifton Webb and Dana Andrews. Preminger's magnificent movie contained a musical theme that has haunted me ever since. It even became a pop song. 'That was Laura, but she's only a dream.'

I was off to find my dream girl in the South Seas. If I was not going to be lucky enough to find Dorothy Lamour in a sarong, I was prepared to settle for a dusky facsimile. To this end, I 'signed on' on the *Queen of Rotarua* – a cargo ship of 10,000 tonnes bound for the inviting blue waters of the Pacific.

If I had gone to a watery grave it would have been with the certain knowledge that *Laura* was better than any British picture I'd ever seen. For life is the stuff that dreams are made of. American film makers have always known that but, with a few exceptions, their British counterparts have never quite got the message.

Life at sea on a small merchantman in the summer of 1945 did not live up to expectations. No Dorothy Lamour, no dusky maidens, not even a South Sea atoll to break the monotony of the empty Pacific which I scanned endlessly with my binoculars. My job as sixth (and last) officer was to keep a day and night lookout for the enemy; the enemy being not only the Jerrys and the Japs but far worse – the Old Man – our ginger nut of a captain. He was rather like James Robertson Justice, the mad skipper in *Doctor at Sea*, only madder! If our three-week journey across the ocean to Oz was tedious it was nowhere near as tedious as that 93-minute movie voyage around the Med, where the sea was as flat as the gags.

If the sea was calm for the location filming above decks, it was pretty rough down below. Lamps swayed, and the crew slipped and slid, as the studio prop men rocked the sets. No continuity, no wit, and a cast all desperately on the lookout for a funny line. You can usually tell where the laughs are supposed to come in a *Doctor* or a *Carry On* film, by listening to the background music. That is often the only way of telling. If you hear the bassoon belching forth on the sound track, you know you should be having a belly laugh. If you hear wah-wah trumpets you know you should be rolling in the aisles. Cymbals and timps are used for pratfalls, while piccolos are usually associated with the private parts.

The instrumental departments worked overtime in that film. Everyone was portrayed as a silly ass. One pities Dirk Bogarde in the title role. *Wimp at Sea* would have been a more fitting title.

Leslie Phillips fared no better in *Doctor in Clover*, where the make-up was as heavy as the humour. Poor Elizabeth Ercy, groomed to be a new Brigitte Bardot, but looking like a Barbie doll, sinks without trace. Everything is reduced to clichés and stereotypes. There are prune jokes and jokes about gay dancers. In fact the ballet receives quite a lot of attention in that one, viz: 'Sorry to bother you, Doctor, but she fell on her entrechat.' And later, when a patient asks a limping ballerina to dance, she replies, 'Certainly, if you wouldn't mind holding my crutch for a moment.'

Then there are the gags about the 'Englishman's Disease':

PATIENT: I was in the trenches bending over to send my men over the top when it went off right up my . . .

DOCTOR: Rectum?

PATIENT: Didn't do 'em any good.

This part of the anatomy is held in high esteem in British comedy.

In *Carry on Nurse* we have a nurse massaging a patient's buttocks and remarking, 'Now we're getting to the bottom of the trouble,' while yet another patient kneeling on the bed with his posterior in the air has the indignity of being photographed with a daffodil stuck where the thermometer should have been.

Pubic hair is also good for a laugh. And, as a male nurse shaves a journalist down there prior to an operation, the wah-wah trumpets work overtime. Then we have a female nurse struggling to remove a shy patient's underpants and remarking, as she finally pulls them off, 'All that fuss over such a little thing.' Believe it or not, those are the absolute highlights. For most of the time we are sitting around on our bedpans waiting for someone to pass the next pooey joke.

The mouldiest of these is the old laughing gas gag, where the patient and surgical staff all roar their heads off as they undertake an excruciatingly painful operation. This I first heard on a gramophone record when I was five years old. It was called *Laughing Gas* and featured our old friend, Jack Hulbert, at the dentist. I didn't laugh then and I didn't laugh now.

I can't remember if we had a doctor on board our little merchantman or not, but, if you are torpedoed, it's better to take a life jacket than a couple of aspirins, unless, of course, you are bobbing about in the water and Jack Hawkins is close at hand in command of a British destroyer. The highlight of *The Cruel Sea* is the moment that Hawkins has to decide whether to rescue the survivors of a sinking merchantman or depth charge the U-boat he suspects is lurking directly beneath them. He takes the hard decision. As things turn out, it is the right one. Black oil surges up to the spot where the survivors were swimming a moment before the explosion. The tension is beautifully maintained by inter-cutting between the various elements involved, and building up to an almost unbearable climax. It was the only moving sequence in yet another film that perpetuates the British wartime myth of puppets in duffel coats, pipes clamped between stiff upper lips, fearlessly facing death and glory in the film studio.

This myth was also pushed in an earlier film by the same director, Charles Frend. In *Scott of the Antarctic* half a dozen thick Brits pull a sled halfway across Antarctica, in order to plant a Union Jack at the South Pole. In the event, they find a Norwegian flag there first, and die of shame. Best thing about the film is its music. Charles Frend obviously knew a good composer when he heard one. Alan Rawsthorne, one of our many grossly underrated composers, served him well in *The Cruel Sea*, while Ralph Vaughan Williams went one better in the *Antarctic*, and composed a symphony to prove it. This monumental work incorporates music from the soundtrack greatly expanded, re-worked and developed. Both scores are extremely evocative. A wind machine and a wordless chorus conjure up icy wastes, and, for once, trumpets and bassoons are not used to dig one in the ribs but to suggest the waddling gait of a Chaplinesque penguin. A mighty organ accompanied by glassy strings becomes a massive glacier. A wistful Romanza brings thoughts of home, while an epic march reminds us of the courage of the explorers, foolhardy though they were. In fact the nobility of the music turns failure into triumph.

But the film itself lacks the imagination of the score. Most of the cast are as wooden as their ski-poles, and there is also a good deal of awkwardness and condescension between the officers and other ranks, with resignation raised to the status of a saintly virtue.

Why do the English love failures? Why are we always celebrating disasters and commemorating them in films such as *A Night to Remember* (the sinking of the *Titanic*) and *Dunkirk*? Is it in order to make us learn by our mistakes and do better next time? If so, the lesson from Scott is obvious. Don't take a hike to the South Pole unless you are prepared to resort to cannibalism when you run out of provisions. Amundsen used huskies and, when he got hungry, just ate the dogs. Making a meal of man's best friend is quite unthinkable to an Englishman.

But from a disastrous event came a great symphony, which stands as a monument to the tenacity of the English race when faced with impossible odds – like trying to get a feature film financed in Great Britain today. Whenever I hear this magnificent symphony I get the image of icy indifference and feel the wind of vicious criticism that is cold enough to freeze the spirit and make all our goals – no matter how misconceived – unachievable. Perhaps we should take a leaf from Amundsen's book and eat the dogs – and we all know who they are.

Not all films about our armed forces deal with heroes. A coward was prominently featured in the Coward epic, *In Which We Serve* – and it wasn't dear Noel. First and foremost this is a chronicle of the life and death of a destroyer from the moment her keel is laid down, until the day she is sunk on active service. Not only did Noel Coward play the captain of the *Torrin* but he also wrote the script, co-directed (with young David Lean) and wrote the music – which was not made into a symphony.

After sinking a troop transport and a German destroyer, all in a night's work, we have the following scene on the bridge as Noel downs a cup of cocoa in the company of Sproggs, his first officer, which sets the tone for much that is to follow:

NOEL: Here comes the dawn of a new day, Sproggs, and I shouldn't be surprised if it were a fairly uncomfortable one.

SPROGGS: Very pretty sky, sir. Someone sent me a calendar rather like that last Christmas.

NOEL: Did it have a Dornier bomber in the top right-hand corner?

SPROGGS: No, sir.

NOEL: That's where art parts from reality.

An exchange like that might be a touch fanciful, but at least it's different from the usual patter one hears on the bridge in the majority of British wartime movies.

As the ship goes down, with all guns blazing and Noel clinging bravely to the binnacle, we have a watery dissolve which takes us back to happier times. After a documentary-type montage of the ship being built and put through her trials, we see Noel say a prayer and sail into action.

After a devastating but successful engagement with the enemy, Noel makes a speech thanking the 243 men of the crew who put on such a jolly good show. The 244th was a craven coward, played by Richard Attenborough, who let the side down by deserting his post at the height of the battle. Noel obviously despised the poor man so much that he didn't even put his name on the credits, not so far as I can see, anyway. Babies and dogs receive an honourable mention but not cowards. Even when he goes on shore leave – alone, of course – Attenborough is not allowed to forget his shame. Even the pianola in the pub where he goes to drown his sorrows is playing 'Run Rabbit, Run'.

The braver members of the crew all go off to their families and friends but even they find it difficult to forget the war. Chief Petty Officer Bernard Miles, in the cinema with his wife, watches the fall of Paris and says, 'Hitler's got France now and France is only twenty miles from England. Makes you think, don't it?'

While OS John Mills, sitting on Plymouth Hoe and gazing out to sea with his working-class girlfriend, Kay Walsh, remarks, 'Funny to think it's such a little island, isn't it?'

'I suppose it is, really,' she replies.

Thus speaketh a typical Noel Coward lower-class moron. But the great man himself, picnicking on the Downs with his wife, Celia Johnson, and the kids, is far truer to himself. As dogfights rage over their heads in decorative white ribbons we eavesdrop on the conversation of the middle class which is equally crass.

CAPT. NOEL: Look Robin, that one diving is a Hurricane.

ROBIN: No, Daddy, it's an ME 109.

CELIA: What a perfectly lovely day it's been, lovely for us, I mean. I suppose that's extremely selfish of me.

CAPT. NOEL: Extremely!

CELIA: I can't believe it's so dreadfully wrong to forget the war now and again, when one can, just for a little.

CAPT. NOEL: I think it's very clever of you, with all hell breaking loose over our defenceless heads.

CELIA: I made the most tremendous effort to make believe it wasn't real at all – they were toys having a mock battle just to keep us amused.

CAPT. NOEL: That's a most shameful confession of pure escapism.

CELIA: I don't care – it has been a lovely day. The sun has been shining and the country looks so green and peaceful.

We'll have to take Celia's word for that, as the film was shot in black and white. Noel Coward spoke like Noel Coward, while Celia Johnson spoke like Celia Johnson, who always spoke the same whatever her class, upper-middle as in *Brief Encounter* or middle-lower as in Coward's *This Happy Breed*. Obviously dear Noel and David Lean loved her for it. The other ranks in *In Which We Serve* spoke mostly cockney, whether they came from Cornwall or Camberwell. It was the done thing. Everything revolved around London. This was a film about 'Hello, darlings' and 'Goodbye, old things', the fortitude of the men at sea and the endurance of the women who stayed behind and were bombed in their homes. But, for all its faults, the film has moments that are genuinely moving, as when a sailor who has just lost his missus as a result of an air raid is glad for his shipmate whose wife miraculously survived in the same house.

End of flashbacks and back to a raft of survivors with someone playing 'Run Rabbit, Run' on the mouth organ and that craven coward Attenborough clinging on for dear life. Moments later, he is machine-gunned, but dies with a smile on his lips as he slips beneath the waves, with Noel's words of consolation ringing happily in his ears. 'Don't worry, I'll write and tell them they should be proud of you.'

Noel himself is picked up by a friendly destroyer with his Number One on board waiting to give him a helping hand and a friendly word.

FIRST OFFICER: We were getting a bit worried about you Skipper.
CAPT. NOEL: Nothing like a good swim before breakfast.

A classic of its kind, all in all, with clever, contrasty photography that transforms the studio tank into the cruel sea. The man responsible was Ronald Neame, who was always a better camera-man than director. Less convincing is Captain Noel's final speech to the survivors: 'Now she [the *Torrin*] lies in 1,500 fathoms and with her more than half of our shipmates. If they had to die, what a grand way to go . . .'

After more of the same, he shakes hands with all the surviving members of his crew, thanking them individually by name. The exceptions are his fellow officers, for by the time he reaches them he can only manage a nod – before choking with emotion and walking off into the fade-out.

Our Captain was a far cry from Coward. He was uncouth and uncool, and feared by most of the crew, including me. Even when the war was over, he made us maintain a round-the-clock lookout for midget submarines. At the time I was too afraid to ask my superiors exactly what they were like. *Above us the Waves* eventually made me something of an authority on the subject.

This was yet another mediocre film extolling another branch of the senior service but there were no females around this time, although there was plenty of talk about them.

FIRST OFFICER: What are you going to do after the war?
SECOND OFFICER: Buy a boat and go sailing.
FIRST OFFICER: Where?
SECOND OFFICER: Anywhere where the booze is cheap and the women have husbands.

(I must admit, I don't quite know how to take that one.) There's also a bit of sucking up to authority by the lower ranks.

OFFICER: Seen any mermaids?
AB: Yes, sir, but they wouldn't look at anything under a commander.

But, in this underwater mini-epic, even the lower orders show their lips can stiffen just as much as those of their superiors. While sneaking through occupied Norway, two ABs dream of the first thing they will do on getting back to England. It's not a tasty bit of crumpet they want but an order of steak and chips with an egg on top. Later, when one lies dying in his mate's arms he manages to stammer out, 'Think you can manage two portions, Fred?'

Is it just the English who are supposed to behave like this, or has it always been thus? Way back in ancient Britain, were the Roman legions sneaking through our swamps dreaming of Fettucini Alfredo? And when one died in his amigo's arms as the result of an ambush did he look into his eyes and say, 'Think you can manage another portion, Federico?' Guessing at the food on offer here in those days I suppose it may well have been possible.

What I dreamed of, on getting back to my country, was an encounter with a woman – not her body but her wrath. What would Mum say when I told her I was not going back to sea? Not wanting me under her feet in the house all day, she actually said, 'Go into your father's business or join the Air Force.' As I didn't want to be fitting shoes on smelly feet for the rest of my life I chose the lesser of two evils – having just tried and failed to get a job as tea boy in the British film industry.

Jack Hulbert and Jessie Matthews – Britain's answer to Fred and Ginger, although they never became partners

Old Mother Riley took the biscuit for boring British comedy

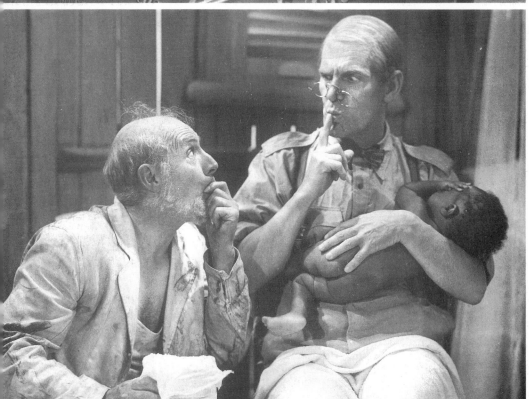

Moore Marriott and Will Hay in *Old Bones of the River*

Malcolm McDowell and Christine Nynan shooting up in Lindsay Anderson's *If*

Uncooperative coeducationalists, Margaret Rutherford and Alastair Sim in *The Happiest Days of Your Life*

Kenneth More in *A Night to Remember*

Scott of the Antarctic, 4 men and a sled

Two things that saved London –
a cup of tea and the Auxiliary Fire
Service. *Fires Were Started*

Boorman's Blitz, *Hope and Glory*

The Cruel Sea

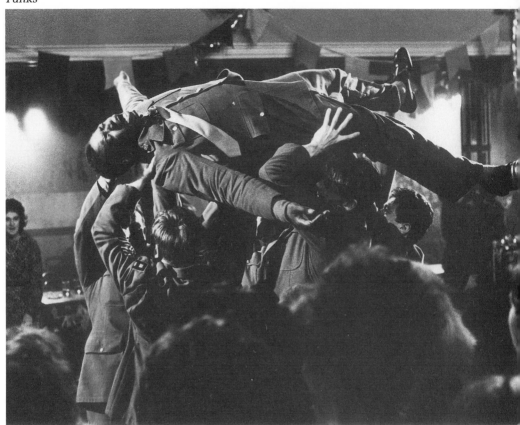

'Dolly Messiter' playing gooseberry in *Brief Encounter*

III

Music in the Air

After the usual square bashing, I was made an electrician and posted to an RAF camp on Salisbury Plain, where I worked in the Acc. room, charging batteries for fighter planes. They were mostly jets but there were still a few old Spitfires around which I looked on with a certain proprietorial interest, as I had helped build them with ticket sales from my film shows in aid of the Spitfire Fund. In the history of the cinema how many British films, I wonder, have featured aeroplanes as their stars?

For one, there was *Target for Tonight*, which featured the Wellington bomber (but that's like comparing a barn owl to a swallow when it comes to the charisma of the Spitfire). 'Never in the field of human conflict was so much owed by so many to so few.' I heard Winston Churchill say that on the radio after the Battle of Britain. And *The First of the Few* showed how the fighter that was largely responsible for that victory came into being. According to the film, it was the brainchild of an aircraft designer called R.J. Mitchell, played here by Leslie Howard, who also directed.

The film starts unpromisingly with ten minutes of maps showing the changing faces of Europe, and newspaper headlines prophesying war. We also learn, over a Wagnerian parody, that the Führer has promised to march to Buckingham Palace at the head of his troops.

Fade-in 'September 15, 1940' . . . and the sky black with model German planes as real British pilots scramble to their fighters and do battle with their phoney lines. As a Spitfire crashes off-screen,

David Niven as Station Commander reflects on its virtues. 'An artistic job, the Spitfire, its designer R.J. Mitchell, a wizard. It all started a long time ago – it must have been 1922 . . .'

Cut to a clifftop where Leslie Howard, dressed in white bags, blazer and boater, is sucking a pipe and watching seagulls. 'Mitch', as he is known to his intimates, is quickly established as an eccentric but affable designer of seaplanes who lives in a studio house built in a studio garden with a studio wife.

There follows a series of shots of model planes flying around a studio sky, as Mitch develops a revolutionary aircraft which eventually wins the coveted Schneider Trophy for the fastest seaplane in the world. He does this against tremendous opposition and meets further resistance when he tells the Air Ministry that England has no adequate defence against the growing might of Germany's Luftwaffe.

By the time he gets the go-ahead to build his dream fighter, he is a sick man with six months to live. However, by working night and day, he begins to realise his ambition. Eventually he is confined to an invalid's chair in his studio garden, which has now sprouted a pool, a rockery, a guest house and a three hundred-year-old oak tree. But, as his studio wife wraps him in a blanket and feeds him soup and sympathy, the first Spitfire flies overhead and into the sunset. Mitch can die a happy man.

Poor Leslie Howard was less fortunate. Having left Hollywood the moment war was declared, he returned to England to make propaganda films. While lecturing on the subject in Portugal in 1943, he delayed his return flight in order to make a personal appearance at the première of *The First of the Few* in Lisbon. The following day, returning to England in a civil aircraft, he was shot down by German fighters over the Bay of Biscay. Portugal was neutral, of course, and this was the only Portuguese plane shot down by the Germans in the entire war. Why? The most likely reason is that pro-Nazi informers had reported that one of the passengers on that ill-fated flight was none other than Winston Churchill, very much incognito. Actually, the man in question was the Churchill lookalike accountant of Leslie Howard.

I have this far-fetched story on the good authority of Lady Walton – widow of the man who wrote the music for the movie. As in the case of *Scott of the Antarctic*, the music was the best thing about *The First of the Few*. The Spitfire Prelude and Fugue by William Walton soon became a concert favourite all over the world. In the film, the prelude accompanied the titles, while the fugue provided the musical structure for a montage showing the genesis of the plane from drawing board to finished fighter. Never has music captured the magic of flight better or the spirit of the genius who created a vehicle in which man and machine become one speeding, soaring entity. The heroism of the pilots is there too, and the certainty of eventual victory in the Battle of Britain.

Composing music for that very subject a quarter of a century later, Walton was not so lucky. Having delivered a finished score for the Saltzman movie, the composer was devastated to learn that Hollywood had chucked it out and commissioned Ron Goodwin (of *633 Squadron* fame) to write a new one. Those who had heard Walton's thrilling music were outraged, particularly Sir Laurence Olivier who played Air Chief Marshal Dowding. It was largely due to his insistence that the original music for one major sequence remained unchanged. That was the 'battle in the air' sequence when for five minutes or so music carries the day and the Luftwaffe is blown out of the Technicolor sky. Once again Walton had been directly responsible for the most memorable moments in the film.

It's not often that British directors realise the power of music and image. They usually rely on words, the stuff of radio and stage plays. But if United Artists were given a nudge by Larry Olivier, himself a great film director, it's hardly surprising. Didn't Olivier commission Walton to write music for his Shakespeare trilogy? And how memorable that music is.

27

Who can ever forget the Battle of Agincourt and the impressive orchestral build-up, as the French knights are lowered into the saddle with block and tackle and set off to charge the lines of their greatly despised foe? Six minutes of mounting tension, expressed in pictures and music, culminating in that magnificent moment when the British yeomen release a thousand arrows simultaneously into the air. A swish in the orchestration makes one's hair stand on end and creates havoc among the ranks of the French as their steeds buck and whinny, and the proud knights in their bright armour hit the ground like tons of multicoloured scrap metal. For once, the achievements of the composer and director are complementary.

Henry V stands as a marvellous example of stylised verismo, which remains pure cinema despite the theatricality. But it is the music that makes the film an entity, the music and Shakespeare's unforgettable verse which blends studio sets based on the *Book of Hours* with the green fields of Ireland, where the battle scenes were shot.

I doubt if the film would work without Walton's evocative music, but the music works without the pictures, as was proved in the Festival Hall in 1990, when a performance of the complete score in the form of a dramatic cantata took place, with Christopher Plummer as narrator.

The music of Patrick Doyle for Kenneth Branagh's film was serviceable rather than memorable. What was the point of a new version, I wondered, as I settled down to watch the 1989 production? What new light could this young upstart throw on this classic play? For the first reel or two I was unimpressed. Unflattering lighting made Branagh look more like Pinocchio than a monarch, and there was a jarring transition from the narrator on a windswept Beachy Head to a studio set purporting to be a castle in Southampton. There was also too much of Falstaff (as was the case in Olivier's version), for his sentimental death means nothing if you are not familiar with *Henry IV, Part 1*. Everyone is weeping and wailing for the passing of a tedious old fart the audience knows nothing about. However, there is a bonus in Branagh's version with the inclusion of an exciting scene where traitors are unmasked and summarily dealt with. That was omitted from Larry's scenario, possibly because the idea of an Englishman betraying his country in the last war was, if not unthinkable, certainly not to be encouraged.

King Henry threatening the Burghers of Calais like a lager lout left me cold, as did the performance of Katharine, with memories of Renee Asherson still very fresh. However, things looked up with the St Crispin Day speech, which was very much in the great British acting tradition and the equal of Olivier's.

The climactic battle scene was probably closer to Flanders than Agincourt, and, apart from a surfeit of slow motion and sword waving, none the worse for that. It deglamorised the battle and brought out the horror of war more tellingly than the earlier version. But it's only natural that the ugly face of battle would be played down in a film made in the grim days of 1943.

Even if Branagh's film doesn't justify constant viewings like the earlier version, in its own rough, tough way it is probably truer to Shakespeare's original than Olivier's more refined effort. And, dare one say it, Branagh makes Olivier seem just an itsy-bitsy camp.

A few shellac discs from the soundtrack of Olivier's film, containing a soliloquy or two and fragments of Walton's score, were constant companions during my sojourn in the Air Force. I frequently played them to my fellow airmen at the Music Circle I ran at Nether Wallop on Salisbury Plain. They enjoyed it as a novelty but their preference was always for Rachmaninov, particularly after the release of Noel Coward's *Brief Encounter*, where it featured heavily on the soundtrack in a serviceable rendition by Eileen Joyce and the National Symphony Orchestra. If memory serves me right, it accompanies the opening credits, which are superimposed on night shots of express trains roaring through a suburban station illuminated by cameraman Bob Krasker's cunningly placed backlights. Then, as the titles come to an end and we cut to a middle-class sitting room in suburbia, we realise that the music is coming from a radio.

Listening to it with an expression bordering on insanity is a middle-aged housewife whose husband does the *Times* crossword every night after dinner.

'Oh, Fred,' Celia manages to blurt out by way of conversation. This sudden outburst shakes Fred to his foundations. Wrenching the pipe from his mouth he replies:

'Darling, what's wrong, what on earth's the matter? Tell me, please.'

'Really and truly, it's nothing,' Celia says, sounding more like dear Noel every moment. 'I had a sort of fainting spell in the refreshment room at Milford. Wasn't it idiotic? Dolly Messiter was with me and she talked and talked and talked till I wanted to strangle her. I suppose she just wanted to be kind; isn't it awful about people meaning to be kind?'

Fred is completely fazed by this and can only say, after a very pregnant pause, 'Would you like to go to bed?'

Even though they have twin beds the very idea horrifies Celia and, before he can move an inch, she stammers, 'No, Fred, really!' Not to be put off he tries a little subtle seduction. 'Come and sit by the fire in the library and relax. You can help me with the *Times* crossword.'

Hardly surprisingly she falls for a handsome stranger who removes a smut from her eye. Compared to Fred he's a passionate Romeo ready to sweep her off her feet. What woman could resist this line of approach – 'My speciality is pneumoconiosis.' Celia's eyes widen in tremulous anticipation. 'Don't be alarmed,' he says reassuringly, 'it's simpler than it sounds. It's nothing but a slow

process of fibrosis of the lung due to inhalation of particles of dust.'
Poor Celia nearly wets herself, and from that moment on is putty in
the handsome doctor's hands. He is also smitten, but the fact that
he, too, is married doesn't help matters. They chase each other over
platforms and share a pot of tea in the station buffet but end up like
trains that pass in the night who never manage to get together for a
little shunting.

Thomas the Tank Engine had more fun than they did. And as
Trevor steams out of her life to a medical practice somewhere in
Africa, Celia chug-chugs off home to Fred, who never seems to
venture out of his cosy engine shed. 'Puff, puff,' he goes on his
pipe. 'You've been a long way away.' Then as their buffers connect
finally with a crash of cymbals, both the film and the concerto
reach their inevitable conclusion. And both are masterpieces of
their kind.

It was at the Music Circle in the RAF that I met the man who was
to change my life. He was a sailor in bell-bottoms, called Boris. He
was an amateur ballet dancer and he was fat, but that didn't stop
him dancing whenever he could or persuading me to do the same.
When I was finally demobbed after two and a half years of skiving,
Bert enticed me to London where he assured me I could earn fame
and fortune as a ballet dancer. I was dubious, and so were my
parents in Southampton. They reminded me that I'd tried to get
work in London once before and failed. And if I couldn't get a job
in films, which I knew something about, how on earth did I expect
to make a career as a dancer? Why, I couldn't even dance the
foxtrot. However, Boris assured them I was a natural and talked
them into giving me a five-pound-a-week living allowance. Up to a
point his faith in me was justified, for, after six months of evening
classes at the Shepherd's Bush Ballet Club, I managed to get a
scholarship at the International Ballet School where I did four
classes a day to make up for lost time. At the age of twenty-one I
was starting ten years too late.

The school was in Queensbury Mews West in South Kensington. There were three boys in the classes and about thirty girls. Nowadays I blush at the lost opportunities for romance but in those days the closest I ever got to a girl was in a pas de deux when I held her around the waist in a supported pirouette. The girls wore black and behaved like cloistered nuns seeking a vocation.

This was a concept that was fostered in the best film on classical ballet ever made – *The Red Shoes*. It was released during my student days and I was there for the very first performance along with a dozen other fans in an otherwise empty cinema at 10 o'clock in the morning at the Odeon, Haymarket. I sat there for two complete screenings, and have seen it at regular intervals ever since. I suppose that anyone other than a ballet aficionado might be mystified by the way in which 'the dance' is elevated to the status of a religion in this film. But to those familiar with the great entrepreneur Sergei Diaghilev on whom Anton Walbrook's impresario was based, it won't seem strange at all. For wasn't it Diaghilev who christened Nijinsky 'the God of the Dance'?

The plot of this Powell and Pressburger production was adopted from a Hans Christian Andersen fairy story about a girl who is given a pair of red ballet shoes by a magician which make her dance until she drops – dead. And, like most good scenarios, it is dead simple. Moira Shearer, a ballerina from the Royal Ballet, plays Vicki Page, and Walbrook plays Boris, a despotic ballet impresario who grooms her for stardom in a production he creates especially for her. Naturally the ballet is called 'The Red Shoes'. And so we are all set for life to imitate art, and vice versa. Having given his acolyte a vocation, as it were, Boris demands total dedication. But when Vicki falls in love with a young composer he feels betrayed and forces her to choose between personal gratification and her art. The resulting conflict in the girl's mind leads to madness and suicide, as indeed it did in the case of the great Nijinsky himself.

The highlight of the film is the 'Red Shoes' ballet with music by Brian Easdale and choreography by one of the masters of his day, Robert Helpmann, who also appears in the film as a soloist. The ballet starts with the Magician, played by Leonide Massine (himself a protégé of Diaghilev), placing the fateful red shoes in his tiny shop window. At once they are seen by an impressionable young girl – Moira Shearer – who is captivated by them. In a flash they are on her feet and she is dancing down the street fit to bust. But when she begins to tire, the red shoes allow her no respite – they have a will of their own and will not be parted from her. Helplessly she dances through time and space, seeking deliverance, but no one can help her until she eventually expires in the arms of a priest who removes her shoes and lays her to rest. That is the end of the ballet. The end of the film is even more harrowing, with the distraught ballerina running off the stage during a performance and out of the theatre, to execute a final grand jeté over a parapet and on to a railway track where a passing express cuts off her feet in their red shoes and brings an end to her torment.

Everything, including Shakespeare, when reduced to a synopsis can sound trite. Certainly *The Red Shoes* is melodramatic and, in the hands of a lesser director, might well have been lacking in taste. The film has a magical quality, but even so, the waves of applause that greet Vicki's first solo actually appearing as giant breakers superimposed on the audience is a little hard to take. And the decor for the ballet also leaves something to be desired with its chocolate box surrealism. But the ballet itself has many imaginative touches, as in a night scene when a swirling newspaper, blowing down a deserted street where Vicki is compulsively dancing, comes to life in the shape of a swirling Bobby Helpmann covered in newsprint, who then joins her in a forlorn pas de deux.

There's also a strangely moving coda in which the apparently cold-blooded Boris Lermontov is shown to have • warm heart. Fighting back the tears, he announces to a hushed audience in front of the curtain that, although Miss Vicki Page will not be appearing tonight, the ballet will still go on. And so it does, with her followspot moving around the stage amongst the characters with whom Vicki would have danced – their reactions eloquently expressing their grief. The last shot in the film is a telling one, with the evil cobbler putting the red shoes back in his window ready to attract the next victim.

Powell also breathes life into the stereotypes involved in the enclosed order of the ballet world and its rigid disciplines. How he ever got the film made remains a mystery. Years later, when I suggested to Harry Saltzman, co-producer of the Bond films, that we do a picture on Nijinsky he snapped back, 'What film on a dancer ever made money?' I couldn't tell him. I doubt if *The Red Shoes* did. Rumour says that its financier, J. Arthur Rank, hated the film and buried it. Thus passed away the first art film in the history of the British cinema. Luckily for us it has been resurrected on video and, after nearly half a century of neglect, there is also available a first-class recording of Easedale's scintillating score.

IV

That's Entertainment: Part 1

I never made it into the International Ballet. After four years of free classes, the authorities decided to cut their losses and kick me out of the school. At twenty-five my technique just wasn't up to the standard demanded of a classical dancer – even in the corps de ballet. However, I was good enough to become a hoofer in the No. 3 Touring Company of *Annie Get Your Gun*. And, whether I was dressed as a cowboy or an Indian, I was in my element. I'd always loved musicals – movie musicals – and now I was actually singing and dancing in a real one. True, it was an American musical – but were there any other sorts in those days? None that I knew of, sad to say. I was soon to change my opinion – a little. A dancer with whom I shared digs dragged me off one afternoon to see *Evergreen*. He was a Jessie Matthews fan and although I protested that the girl with the plum in her mouth had no appeal and that I'd seen the film at Pangbourne, he convinced me that I should have another look. What else was there to do on a wet Monday afternoon in Sheffield, anyway?

He was right. I was wrong – almost. Most musicals have slim plots and this was no exception. It took mistaken identity as its theme. So forget the story about Jessie impersonating her mother making a comeback after mysteriously disappearing at the height of her career as a popular music hall star (in order to bring up her illegitimate daughter) and let's get on with the singing and dancing.

One of the most memorable moments in the 'Cavalcade of

Dance' sequence is set in the Great War and features a *ballet mécanique* (reminiscent of the expressionist choreographer, Kurt Joss) in which a line of chorus girls pass along an assembly line to be manufactured into a batch of high explosive shells. There is more than a flavour of *Metropolis* in the sets here, while the score reminds me of the Machines music Arthur Bliss produced for *Things to Come* around the same time.

Next came the 'Jazz Age' with Jessie doing a wild Charleston with super long legs, followed by the highlight of the film, the 'Dancing on the Ceiling' number, where she yearns for her lover, asleep in the room below. With an inspired chiffon dress floating around her in voluminous gossamer clouds, she drifts around the room like a reincarnation of Isadora Duncan with a suspicion of Ginger Rogers. But, truth to tell, she's really her own woman, as when she dances up a curving staircase with a succession of tiny little-girl hops and chorus-girl high kicks interspersed with amazing back bends. Exuding charm and grace she pirouettes around her light and airy art deco room then leaps on to the bed – landing in a perfect arabesque. Although she seems to be moving in dreamy slow-mo, her dance is actually in real time. It's just that her ingenious costume, combined with her natural artistry and the soft focus camerawork of Glen Mac Williams, create that illusion. And, of course, one must not forget the individual choreography of Buddy Bradley – Britain's answer to Busby Berkeley.

Jessie had an engaging way with a song and, apart from her accent, which I guess they could have fixed, she was the equal of many a Hollywood star with the advantage of a big publicity machine behind them. And Jessie had something they did not have – a nymph-like sexuality.

I once saw her perform at the Music Hall in Santa Monica, just down the road from the studios in Hollywood. She was still in a voluminous dress but at seventy or so, Jessie had grown rather voluminous herself. And I'm afraid she was still 'Dancing on the

Ceiling' – or trying to, poor love. She should have followed her stage mother's example in *Evergreen* and retired, while she was still ahead of the game.

After *Evergreen* she made a couple of unmemorable musicals and then more or less faded into oblivion. More unmemorable British song and dance movies followed without her. We also produced a succession of hybrid musicals set in Britain with a succession of transatlantic stars such as David Niven and Vera Ellen. Despite the obvious talents involved, these films don't bear thinking about. And when we did attempt to cultivate the home-grown variety, it wilted and died.

One such specimen was *London Town*, featuring Sid Field, a fading variety artiste, in some tired old music hall routines, and a dozen and one 'beautiful' girls in tight perms, garish make-up and lime-green gowns. It was a tourist's nightmare with city-types jiving in Trafalgar Square and pearly Kings and Queens doing cockney capers on 'Amstead 'Eath. There were hosts of plastic daffs in Hyde Park, two hundred swans on a studio Thames and Two-Ton Tessie O'Shea flying off a swing and falling among a lot of punts at Windsor. *London Town* was an indigestible Technicolor trifle, served up by a hundred crooners and ten pianists bashing away at a gigantic concert grand producing some of the sickliest music ever heard.

Modern London has never fared very well in musicals – one has only to think of *Absolute Beginners*. The metropolis seems to have come off best with musicals set in the past. *Oliver!* is a good example. Music by Lionel Bart; Production Design, John Box; Cinematography, Ozzy Morris; Director, Carol Reed. Now you're talking. Frankly I've never heard of the choreographer, Onna White, but she did a great job. All in all it was a fine combined effort by cast and crew alike. Take 'Consider Yourself One of the Family'. Here we had a cross section of London types that for once were out of Mayhew's *London Labour and the London Poor* rather than a picture postcard stand at Piccadilly Circus. It was an authentic-looking bit of cockney history come to life with 'Peelers' dancing with washerwomen and porters dancing with sides of beef at Smithfield. We had newspaper boys and comic street dancers; we had little sweeps cooling their arses in a horse trough; we had bottle cleaners and brick layers, brewers trundling barrels, costermongers pushing carts of cabbages and fishwives doing a clog dance at Billingsgate – and not one token American tourist in sight. The entire sequence is a cinematic triumph, ending in a spectacular overhead crane shot showing everyone doing their own thing in song and dance.

Equally good is the 'Who Will Buy This Wonderful Morning' number, in which young Oliver looks out of a high window in a posh town house at the goings-on in the spacious square below – a real kid's-eye view of a wonderful world that is entirely new to him. Window cleaners slide up and down their ladders, house-maids beat rugs, nursemaids dance with prams and school-teachers shoo crocodiles of children around the pond. Once again, the movement is born from within the characters themselves and the everyday tasks they perform – not from a Broadway dance studio. The film isn't perfect – what film ever is? The scenes of brutality do not sit comfortably alongside the comedy scenes and there are too many longueurs between numbers – but for all that we have a good ethnic rough and tumble and a subtle use of colour which enhances the mood of every scene, be it sunny or sombre. And not a whiff of Hollywood anywhere.

Back to me masquerading as a cowboy in Sheffield. The curtain rang down on *Annie* for the last time on what had been a three-year run for most of the cast and a three-week run for me.

On returning to London I auditioned for *Brigadoon* and failed. I didn't care much – I look rather bogus in a kilt. After a few more abortive efforts I decided to give up the dance before it gave up me.

And, because I was a tolerable mime, I decided to take up acting. Accordingly I went for an audition with the Garrick players of Newton Poppleford. I got the job. I was the only applicant. One of the plays in the weekly repertory was *When Knights Were Bold*, a film I remembered seeing as a cadet. It featured Jack Buchanan –yet another dancing Brit who deserved better material than he usually got. He was handsome, debonair, and had a lazy way with a tap routine that was surprisingly sexy.

The best thing about *Knights* is a nostalgic soft-shoe number Jack dances alone in a dusty dungeon dressed, as always, in impeccable (dust-free) white tie and tails. I suppose he really was England's answer to Fred Astaire. They shared the same easy charm and it was good to see them starring together in the best film Jack ever made – *The Band Wagon*. Yes, it took Hollywood to deploy his talents to the full in a wide-screen musical where he was brilliantly cast as an eccentric Broadway director, well able to upstage the other members of the starry cast, including Fred himself. For me he had the best line in the film, 'Men in armour, light your chandeliers!' But he was best of all as a bonnie baby of seven months in the showstopping 'Triplets' number – what a performance for someone nearing seventy.

My performance in *When Knights Were Bold* was so bad that I was relegated to playing a ghost in a suit of armour that walked as the curtain fell at the end of Act I – after forty-five minutes of painful immobility. Bankruptcy followed as the play flopped after a week of incessant rain in the Redout Gardens, Teignmouth. As an actor I was a washout.

V

Goodbye to Ealing

Having failed to become a director, a dancer or an actor I decided to try my hand at photography. If nothing else, I had learned over the years that, whatever their talents, show biz folk always need flattering portraits. The fact that I happened to know a photographer who taught at the South West Essex Technical College and School of Art (known locally as Walthamstow Tech) was a great help. I got a scholarship quite easily and, with the aid of another hand-out from Dad, started yet another student course at the age of twenty-six. Part of the curriculum included snapping studies of London and Londoners, and this in turn aroused my interest in how London was portrayed in our films. Cinematically, the capital appeared to be inhabited by a handful of well-known lookalikes. Stanley Holloway seemed to live here, there and everywhere, as did Alfie Bass, Naunton Wayne and Basil Radford.

Alec Guinness got about quite a lot too, as did Sydney Tafler and Margaret Rutherford. But whether the location was Lavender Hill, Kentish Town, Pimlico or Mayfair, it was usually the same set revamped on the back lot at Ealing Studios. The characters were interchangeable. Most of these films were weak situation comedies in search of an identity. The unlikely bank clerk of Alec Guinness and the unconvincing artist of Stanley Holloway living in a fading hotel among sweet old ladies in bootees and straw boaters would be equally unbelievable in Camden Hill, Haverstock Hill, Beulah Hill or any other hill outside the Studios where most of them were manufactured. The stories were also pretty far-fetched, with petty criminals turning out model Eiffel Towers made of stolen gold bullion in a deserted factory down the road. *Passport to Pimlico* made in 1949 was nearly as phoney.

We open on a painted sky, which may have looked wonderful in colour but looks wishy washy in black and white. The camera then pulls back through an open window into a nondescript room where an electric fan is whirring. We see a foreign-looking man. He is hot and sweaty. Latin-American music plays on the soundtrack, suggesting that we are south of the border. The man looks out of the window down on to a flat roof where a pretty girl in a bikini is sunbathing. The camera glides past her and down a striped awning to reveal a fishmonger's and shire horses pulling carts.

But, as the chimes of Big Ben ring out, we realise that we are not in tropical climes but in London town in the throes of a heatwave. To underline the obvious, we see newspaper headlines of the 'Temperature Soars' variety and everyone in shirtsleeves, mopping their brows. So far we have not moved out of the Studios where even the street is a badly lit set. We are then introduced to the locals, including a fat policeman warning the cast about an unexploded bomb that has just been discovered on a nearby bomb site. Among the old familiar faces is John Slater, the local fishmonger, who has obviously done well for himself as he has stopped being a barrow boy in the East End and moved up West, or to be more exact, South West. Judging from his long face and vacant look he doesn't seem too happy about it.

We now cut to the Town Hall where Stanley Holloway, a local do-gooder we last saw as a baddie in Lavender Hill, is trying to convince the Council that they should turn the bomb site into a kids' playground and swimming pool. In this he is opposed by the majority of the Councillors who, being hard-nosed businessmen, want to sell it.

The bomb goes off, revealing a secret cache of buried treasure –

together with an ancient charter signed by King Edward IV ceding the land that is now known as Pimlico over to the Duke of Burgundy for services rendered; a Royal Act that has never been revoked. Realising that they are no longer subject to the laws of England, the new Burgundians shout, 'Blimey, I'm a foreigner,' and tear up their ration books, throw away their clothing coupons, and sing, 'Knees up Mother Brown' all night long at the pub on the corner. It is about now that we begin to realise that there are no teenagers around and that we are watching yet another middle-aged Ealing comedy. True, there are a few kids – but purely as nuisance value.

The usual Ealing Battle is waged between the close-knit little community (in an assortment of garments worthy of Oxfam) and the miserable Men From The Ministry sporting bowler hats and briefcases. This eventually results in the children being evacuated and the new Burgundians being in a state of siege and starving to death. This is where the kids come to the rescue. On seeing a keeper in London Zoo feeding the seals, they get the bright idea of throwing food over the barbed wire to their beleaguered parents. Their example soon bears fruit as busload after busload of extras arrive to do likewise.

It is something of a convention in Ealing comedies that when the going gets tough, a band of uncomprehending extras appear from nowhere and proceed to save the day. This was even the case in one of the later Ealing efforts, shot in colour: *The Titfield Thunderbolt*. As usual, the tired old script was by T.E.B. Clarke and featured hugely inappropriate music by Georges Auric, a lightweight Parisian composer, whose sophisticated British film scores never succeeded in losing their French accent.

Once again the film examines the conflict between a tight little community – in this case a village – and the Men From The Ministry, who close down the oldest surviving branch line in the world and the station that serves it. But the elders of the village, in the shape of the vicar and the squire, refuse to take the situation lying down and conspire to open a communal railway of their own – providing they can raise the money for it.

Traditional means of extorting money from the gullible British Yeoman are all brought into play – a performance of *The Mikado*, a raffle, a jumble sale, a fête, a silver collection in church. After which they are still £10,000 short. Enter Stanley Holloway. Again. Having moved from Lavender Hill to Pimlico, he has now retired to the country, where a surfeit of Ealing comedies seem to have driven him to drink. This time we find him propping up the bar of the local. As he appears to be as affluent as he is alcoholic, the squire touches him for a donation. At first Stanley appears uninterested, but, when he learns that there will be a bar on the 9.15 and he will be able to start drinking one hour and forty-five minutes earlier than usual, he quickly chips in.

Now comes the usual general meeting in the Village Hall with the Men From Whitehall. Also bidding for the franchise for a new service is a local bus company full of baddies. In the event, the railway enthusiasts get a conditional go-ahead for a limited period. The dilapidated railway has to be spruced up and set in motion. Enter the extras, who, for reasons relating to the budget, are wearing their own towny-type clothes. Without pausing for breath, they hang pots of geraniums, stick up posters and paint the station from one end of the platform to the other. Then they achieve a feat unequalled since the building of the pyramids in Cecil B. DeMille's *Ten Commandments* – they manhandle a massive engine shed from one end of the station yard to the other. And, even though it is all in long shot, so that it is impossible to see their bulging eyes, one can certainly see their buckling bandy legs and ape-like arms. The rupture count must have been remarkably high. After this they all disappear – probably to hospital – the train gets under way and Stanley gets pissed.

Now it is the baddies' turn. And the scriptwriter falls back on another stalwart – the steam traction engine. This splendid machine was once the star of the comedy in its own right, but here it has only a supporting role and in a head-on clash of the titans at a level crossing it is ignominiously vanquished while the train steams on in triumph.

The drunken, pheasant-shooting fireman precipitates the next hazard by accidentally puncturing a water tower with his double barrel shotgun. How to get water to top up the tank? Enter the extras again as fifty unlikely passengers jump out of the carriages and head for the local farm to pillage every water-carrying device they can lay their hands on, from bedpans to hip baths. And although they seem to spill more than they save, the replenished engine is soon chugging off – leaving behind a battlefield of containers.

Before long, the village railway is running at a profit until, one dark night, the train is derailed and destroyed by the baddies. Enter the extras once more. They raid the local museum and steal the Titfield Thunderbolt, an engine of similar vintage to Stephenson's Rocket. But an Ealing extra's work is never done. Next they borrow the drunken fireman's home – a Victorian railway carriage – and, almost on their knees, carry it through field and pasture to the station, where they unearth some wheels and spruce it up for the Minister's visit. With stopwatch in hand, he sits aboard the chugging train, watched anxiously by the village elders, as it is put through its paces. All seems to be going well until an emergency stop snaps a makeshift coupling, parting the engine from its carriages. Here, for the very last time, the extras save the day, by jumping out to perform their most herculean task – pushing the carriage up a steep incline towards the stationary engine. They simply had to halt the film there – otherwise I am sure the extras would have gone on strike. In fact I often wondered, as I confronted a bolshie crowd of extras years later, if it wasn't this experience that turned them into such an objectionable bunch.

However, that particular generation have all retired to antique supermarkets. The new breed are 'ace'.

Oh yes, the train freaks get their franchise . . . by default. Thinking their super slow journey of 24.8 mph between A and B will prove their downfall, they eventually discover that it is their salvation. Twenty-five mph would have exceeded the speed limit permissible on a light railway system.

And so the Ealing comedians win the day. They win in Pimlico too, after a fashion. They surrender their independence and their treasure trove in exchange for new ration books and a super recreation centre for the kids. Starting a comedy is always easier than bringing it to a satisfactory conclusion.

The very last Ealing comedy of all was the most successful in this regard with all the cast except one ending up *dead*. Did *The Ladykillers* kill off the Ealing comedies for good? If so it was a gloriously black way to go.

We are still in London and there is still a conflict between good and evil. The good is a little old lady and the evil is a bunch of crooks using her abode in King's Cross as a safe house for a daring bank robbery. The trouble starts when she tumbles their little game and turns the tables – so that they end up six feet under and she ends up counting the loot. It was such a good film that its director, Sandy Mackendrick, went straight to Hollywood and never came back.

Two points in its favour were that the script was not by Tubby Clarke and the music was not by Georges Auric. Sandy (aided by his cameraman 'Crazy' Otto Heller) made London look like London and not a crummy film set. In this the film had something in common with *Hue and Cry*, the very first of the Ealing comedies. *Hue and Cry* was also the first of Tubby Clarke's bomb site scripts – absolutely brimming over with naughty kids scampering through blitzed buildings to flush out a gang of crooks and bring them to justice. Once again it was the extras to the rescue – legions of them.

As Charles Crichton, the director, was also responsible for *The Titfield Thunderbolt*, could it be that these unsuspecting kids were the selfsame extras he was already training to fetch and carry that heavy rolling stock all those years later?

It wasn't till much, much later that I saw a comedy in which London was an integral part of the story and not just a convenient backdrop. And the characters themselves really belonged too – they weren't just the same old faces doing the same old thing in a different district. The film was called *The Optimists of Nine Elms* and must have won the 'Worst Title of the Year' award of 1973. But strangely enough it didn't win the Best Actor of the Year Award, despite a virtuoso performance by Peter Sellers.

He plays a misanthropic street musician down on his luck, who barely scrapes together enough to feed himself and his only friend, a scruffy mongrel. Enter two neglected kids, equally scruffy, who live in a nearby slum. Dad's too busy earning and Mum's too busy with the new baby to bother with them. But at least they have each other and a potential friend in Sellers whom they follow around the streets as he plays for pennies. He tolerates the children but is not easily won over. They call him 'Mister', he calls them 'Nothing'. He lives in a squalid squat with few creature comforts and the kids don't fare much better – they haven't a toy between them and have to empty their potty in the one and only outside loo every morning and wash under the kitchen tap. But are they downhearted? No! Why? Because they live in hope of moving to a new block of council flats with a little dog to keep them company.

One day they take Sellers to the water's edge and point out the celestial towers gleaming through the sunny mist of the Thames on the far shore. Gradually, and against his better judgement, Sellers guardedly opens up to the kids, whom he recognises as outcasts like himself, and grudgingly decides to help them. He suggests they baby-sit his sick mongrel to earn a bit of pocket money while he slips out for a pint. This will enable them to buy a dog of their own at Battersea Dogs' Home. They jump at the idea and soon have enough saved up to buy a pup which they take home in triumph. Their parents go crazy. Dad says no pets are allowed in the flats where they are going and even shows the kids a notice nailed to the wall to prove it. They've got the flats mixed up anyway. They are not headed for the posh ones on the far side of the river but the old ones on the wrong side of the river.

Meanwhile Sellers' mongrel dies and he gets slowly blotto as the kids bury the body in the dogs' cemetery in Kensington Gardens in the dead of night. When Dad discovers the kids have gone missing he nearly goes demented until he is finally put on their trail by Sellers. But when Dad arrives at the graveyard there is no sign of them and his anxiety deepens until – come the dawn – he finds them peacefully sleeping beneath a bush. A touching reconciliation follows and then they are off to their new home while Sellers gets their dog and the Horse Guards go riding by.

Told with economy and sensitivity, this underrated film establishes Tony Simmons as a first-rate director and justifies the risk Sellers took in tackling a difficult role in an offbeat subject and doing it for peanuts. It was one of his last films and one of his best. The rest of the cast also turned in convincing portrayals. *The Optimists of Nine Elms* was a great achievement all round, with an extra special word of praise for the editor, Jimmy Jympson. And if you need convincing that he's one of the best around, just look at the scene where the little girl loses her littler brother on a refuse site by the river's edge. Screaming gulls, the snapping jaws of the excavator, the rushing river and screeching trains intercut with the growing panic on the girl's face, all combine to produce an almost unbearable tension. And how refreshing to meet some real Londoners, resilient, dogged, philosophic, with a wry sense of humour second to none.

I wonder what sort of film Tony Simmons would make in Nine Elms now.

VI

Return to Ealing

Notting Hill Gate was my stamping ground in the days when, having finished my studies at Walthamstow Tech, I was finding my feet as a freelance photo-journalist. That was around the time of the Festival of Britain when Joe Orton was also knocking around the same area. In fact we may have been living in the same block, if the film of *Prick Up Your Ears* is to be believed. Could it be that, as Joe Orton was in bed with his boyfriend watching the Coronation on TV, I was using the same event, almost next door, as an excuse to get my new girlfriend to stay away overnight for the first time in her life. Bloody disaster, as it turned out, both for me and Joe Orton. Gary Oldman as the gay genius turned in a remarkable performance, managing the transition from ingenuous provincial lad to glam metropolitan sophisticate with an invisible technique. Far more convincing than the director's evocation of the Festival of Britain site down by the Thames – more like *Spring in Park Lane* than sodomy on the South Bank, my dears!

One of Orton's plays, *Entertaining Mr Sloane*, was turned into a film, which used one of my favourite cemeteries as its key location. All budding photographers turn to graveyards sooner or later for inspiration. I remember photographing my first wife dressed up as Charlotte Brontë on our honeymoon in the churchyard at Haworth in Yorkshire – but that's another story.

Back to Brompton Road and *Mr Sloane*, which was made at the end of the Swinging Sixties, a time when film production in Britain was at its most flamboyantly productive – simply because the

American financiers were convinced that *here* was where it was all happening. At that moment in time maybe it was. It was the time of 'Anything Goes'. The idea of raising money in this day and age for such a wacky story would be utterly unthinkable, especially with such an offbeat cast.

Joe Orton's stage play was a knockout. I can't remember who played the sex-starved sister but the sinister Pete Vaughan played her homosexual brother while Dudley Sutton played the blond Adonis in black leather who 'comes' between them. But what works as an offbeat black comedy in the theatre fails to grip in the cinema where the darkness is made light. The direction becomes as brash as the dayglo colours of Beryl Reid's see-through mini-dress. And although Harry Andrews was gay in real life, he fails to convince us on the screen, despite his camp little hat and pink Cadillac. He is as understated as his sister Beryl is over the top. Caught in between, poor Peter McEnery just doesn't know which way to turn, performance-wise. The plot, such as it is, turns on who will win the tug of war for Peter's penis before he gets tired of playing pig-in-the-middle and buggers off. In the event he murders Beryl's and Harry's Dad, who manages the churchyard surrounding the Gothic folly in which most of the sex-play takes place. This indiscretion enables the brother and sister to blackmail Mr Sloane into shacking up with them in a bisexual *ménage à trois*, until death do them part.

As the 'Swinging Sixties' became the 'Silly Sixties' similar indulgences, like *Modesty Blaise*, began to sound the funeral knell on the zany style that was probably brought into existence when Dick Lester first shouted 'Action'! on day one of his second Beatles epic, *Help*! What's the line from that famous song of theirs – 'Nothing is real'? But for all their faults, at least these films, good and bad alike, were trying to break new ground.

Back in the early Fifties when I was struggling to make a living as a photographer, Britain was still cultivating the same old soil so far as comedy was concerned. I remember a certain photo agency suggesting I go along to Hyde Park where a film was being shot which featured the London to Brighton Veteran Car Rally. The film was called *Genevieve*. When I arrived I noticed to my horror that I was wearing a suit of exactly the same material as Kay Kendall, the star. It was a mustard-flecked Donegal tweed. She noticed it too and was not amused. Neither was I when I finally saw the film. Here was the director, Henry Cornelius, up to his old tricks, mixing studio and location work as he had in *Passport to Pimlico*. All the long shots of the ancient cars setting off were filmed in Hyde Park and all the close-ups on a sound stage at Pinewood. The mood and atmosphere are completely different and the light doesn't match. Maybe audiences were less sophisticated then. Now you only have to watch 'Points of View' on BBC TV to realise that your average viewer is not only an expert in continuity but can also tell travelling matte from back projection.

Genevieve delighted millions – but not me. For a start I had trouble with the barrister's wife, Wendy – not because she doesn't share her husband's enthusiasm for getting into a fifty-year-old car and taking two days to drive to Brighton and back, but because she's such a twit. She lives in a dinky mews cottage in Belgravia, but a mere knock at the door is enough to make her drop eggs and onions. For some reason she does her housework in lemon-coloured kid gloves and is at her wits' end because the cleaners have pressed the pleats in her skirt the wrong way round.

However, she serves sherry all round when her husband – John Gregson, playing truant from Ealing – presents her with an Edwardian motoring hat. (Gregson is something of a curator in the museum of British comedy when it comes to old crocks and even older cracks.) The other people, in what turns out to be a private race to Brighton, are Kenneth More and the Lady in my Donegal tweed – Kay Kendall – who make a far more racy couple than the folks who live in the mews. But alas, their dialogue is not exactly high octane. 'Do you know,' confides More to Gregson, re Kendall, 'for a long time she wouldn't eat anything but ravioli – isn't that strange?'

And so we bump and bang and backfire our way to Brighton, aided and abetted by the tuneful harmonica of Larry Adler. Infectious as the *Genevieve* theme undoubtedly is, it does begin to pall a bit after the thirty-ninth repeat.

In Brighton we have a crummy hotel with a chiming clock outside the bedroom window, and Kay Kendall trying to kid us that she is playing a swing version of 'Genevieve, Sweet Genevieve' on the trumpet. Miming like that wouldn't even fool a weeny-bopper these days. Then both couples get drunk and race back to London again, by which time I seem to remember that someone is pregnant.

The best performance comes from Kenneth More – I used to live next door to him – exactly the same off-screen as on, charming! I suppose charm was what *Genevieve* was all about. Around this time British films were very high on charm. Officers in the forces had it to a man and no one living in the West End was ever without it. Commuters north of the Thames sometimes had it while the unfortunates south of the river seldom had it. People from the East End never had it. J. Arthur Rank, the film and flour mogul, dreamed of making a fortune by exporting it on celluloid and opened a Charm School for that very purpose. As long as the encyclopedia of cockney rhyming slang exists J. Arthur will be fondly remembered.

This was the era of the Teddy Boy – a lower-class lad who aspired to Edwardian sartorial elegance, with sideburns and winkle-pickers. The most flamboyant styles were to be found in Brixton, so I spent a lot of time there snapping material for my photo essay on the Teddy Boy phenomenon.

With its bustling street market winding beneath the railway bridge, Brixton struck me as an exciting location for a discerning film maker in search of a unique corner of London. By the time it was used, Teddy Boys were as rare as vintage cars.

Brixton has become a no-go area – at least according to *Sammy and Rosie Get Laid*, a film by Stephen Frears. Despite the superficial violence, what we have here is good escapist entertainment of the 'England That Never Was' variety, as fanciful in its way as *Passport to Pimlico*. In this case those being evicted from their homes – some of them mobile – reminded me more of the characters in that great 1933 musical *Roman Scandals*. But in the American movie the homes of the dispossessed are to be pulled down to make room for a new jail, while in the British movie the victims' houses are being bulldozed away to make room for a new motorway.

Civilisation has evidently progressed since the Eddie Cantor movie. In *Roman Scandals* the people owned their homes. In the Frears film they are squatters on private property, with no right to be there in the first place. The American film has better music too, and better lyrics – who can ever forget 'Keep Young and Beautiful'? The best the British can manage is 'I Vow To Thee My Country', a poor man's 'Land Of Hope And Glory'. The most memorable musical number in the Frears film is when a beautiful American photographer, who leads a charmed life, dances gracefully among the mêlée of policemen wielding batons and protesters throwing petrol bombs.

There is little 'charm' in this film. Instead we have the 'Smirk', that says 'I know best, asshole!' It often accompanies lectures on the evils of our society and that's what we get here, ad nauseam, from our hectoring couple. Yes, Sammy and Rosie get laid all right, but never hatch into real human beings.

My Teddy Boy series photographed in Brixton sold rather well and soon I'd saved enough to start making amateur movies. They cost money and they took time, neither of which I could afford, with a mortgage to pay off and a growing family to support. Three years later and three films later I felt ready to be taken seriously – hadn't I just won the prestigious 'Amateur Movie Maker' Film of the Year Award? But whom to dazzle? A friend suggested Norman Swallow, the Assistant Head of Films at the BBC. I sent him my films and he sent for me.

I duly arrived at Ealing Studios, which had been bought up by the BBC. Fifteen years earlier, I'd been politely but firmly turned away when I told the commissionaire that I would like to become a film director but would settle for tea boy. However, Ealing films had come and gone. Ultimately, like *The Titfield Thunderbolt*, they ran out of steam. The big screen was being swallowed up by the small screen. It was my hope that television would be less of a closed shop, less of an old boy network.

Norman Swallow liked my work and promised to push it in the direction of Huw Wheldon, the editor of a new Arts programme, 'Monitor'. Wheldon eventually interviewed me in Stage 6 at Ealing (the Red Lion Pub). A week later he summoned me to Lime Grove Studios at Shepherds Bush to give me the verdict.

VII

The Death of Gainsborough

The interview with Wheldon at Ealing had not gone well and it was with some trepidation that I approached yet another pair of studio gates which had been shut firmly against me in the past. For this was once the home of Gainsborough Films. You may remember their logo (which crops up from time to time on TV) – a picture in a gilded frame of a lady in a period costume wearing a big hat with ostrich feathers. And whereas the MGM lion turns to the audience and roars, the Gainsborough Lady gives us a condescending nod and a simpering smile. This was symptomatic of their product which included a veritable procession of ladies in kitsch period clothes and feathered hats, some simpering like Pat Roc, others pouting like Margaret Lockwood in *The Wicked Lady*. You could tell the good from the bad by the amount of cleavage displayed. La Lockwood won by miles. Not only was her dress cut daringly low for those days, but her breasts were pushed alarmingly high to boot. And talking of boots, she wore those as well – right up to the thigh as a bold highwaywoman.

By day she is the demure wife of Sir Ralph Thingamabob, a country magistrate who has longer hair than her ladyship and is a bit of a sissy. After dark, the wicked lady dons a mask and menswear and takes to the road. She starts on this life of crime after gambling away a treasured heirloom which she manages to retrieve by holding up the coach in which the new owner of the precious bauble is travelling home. This gives her a taste for the excitement missing from a humdrum life with his wimpish lordship. She only married him anyway to spite Pat Roc, her goody-goody cousin to whom he was already betrothed. Enter James Mason as a fellow highwayman, called Captain Jack, who becomes her new partner, both on the road and in the four-poster. But on finding him in the arms of another doxy one dark night, she betrays him and turns up at Tyburn to see him swing. But he escapes and lives to ride again – both his gallant steed and the wicked lady herself, whom he takes against her will, without even removing his spurs. These acts of passion are conducted through long overcoats buttoned to the ankle and layer upon layer of linen and winter underwear. The only articles of clothing the lovers remove are their ostrich-feathered hats, and there is always a tasteful fade-out as they kiss and hit the horizontal.

At the scriptwriter's insistence, the faithless pair become partners in crime again until the going gets tough and the wicked lady shoots Captain Jack in the back. She also shoots a trusty servant and poisons and smothers an aged retainer – less because he threatens to reveal her guilty secret, than because he wants to save her soul. So she's not all bad; and there is a corner of her hard heart that has a soft spot for a mysterious stranger who turns up from time to time, and the last time blows her away with a ball from his stout musket.

Great stuff, the stuff of cult movies and midnight screenings, with the kids applauding each new betrayal and every banal line of dialogue.

The success of *The Wicked Lady* inspired Gainsborough to produce a spate of similar epics, usually starring Maggie Lockwood playing her same wicked self. *The Man in Grey* and its Technicolor remake, *Jassy*, spring to mind. The dialogue too was interchangeable, as were the pearls of wisdom – viz, 'The world would be a better place if people loved each other more.' Formula stuff with no surprises; the good are very, very good and rather dumb but wise up in the last reel to triumph over the very, very wicked, who get their comeuppance towards the end. The last scene of all shows true love prevailing, as the lovers engage in a chaste embrace and cascading false hair from their Restoration wigs voluptuously intertwines.

As I waited in a corridor outside one of the studios for the boss of 'Monitor' to appear, there wasn't a plumed hat in sight. Everything had been auctioned off, and the Restoration finery returned to the theatrical costumiers. Where extras once jostled together on their way to the set, producers and PAs from the Talks Department hurried to get their shows on the air – current affairs programmes like 'Tonight' and 'Panorama', programmes packed with hot news and human interest – a million miles away from the never-never world of the black mask and the well-placed beauty spot.

Then, along came the Editor of 'Monitor', the first regular arts programme in the history of British television, possibly the world. Despite my poor showing at the interview, Huw Wheldon found some of my ideas quite promising. More important, he couldn't get my film *Amelia and the Angel* out of his mind. He had decided to give me a crack to replace his best film director.

After working on the programme for a year or so, John Schlesinger, whose documentaries I had much admired, was off to make his first feature film. Adapted from a novel by Stan Barstow, *A Kind of Loving* examines the morals and mating habits of a young working-class couple in a dreary Northern town.

We open on snotty-nosed kids playing in a slum. It looks like Salford. Across the road a wedding group is posing for a photograph on the steps of a church black with grime. We are in the grip of winter and surrounded by debris and desolation. And so the scene is set for a screen romance between June Ritchie – an envious face in the crowd – and Alan Bates, a member of the wedding who catches her eye. The only thing they have in common is their workplace – a vast, anonymous factory where they spend their drab lives dreaming of other things, like sex, sex

Henry V by Branagh *(inset), Henry V* by Olivier. Blood and guts versus the Book of Hours

Passport to Pimlico. Nothing to declare

Carry on Nurse. Bedpan humour

The Titfield Thunderbolt

Two-ton Tessie O'Shea in *London Town*

Left: Alec Guinness melting gold bullion in *The Lavender Hill Mob.* Another nice little earner for Ealing

Below: The Red Shoes. Ballet puts J. Arthur Rank in the red

Above: Oliver. Britain's best-ever musical

Left: The Optimists of Nine Elms. One of Peter Sellers' best characterisations. The dog wasn't bad either

Genevieve. Breakdown on the Brighton Road

The Lady Killers

Entertaining Mr Sloane

Prick Up Your Ears   *Overleaf: Modesty Blaise*

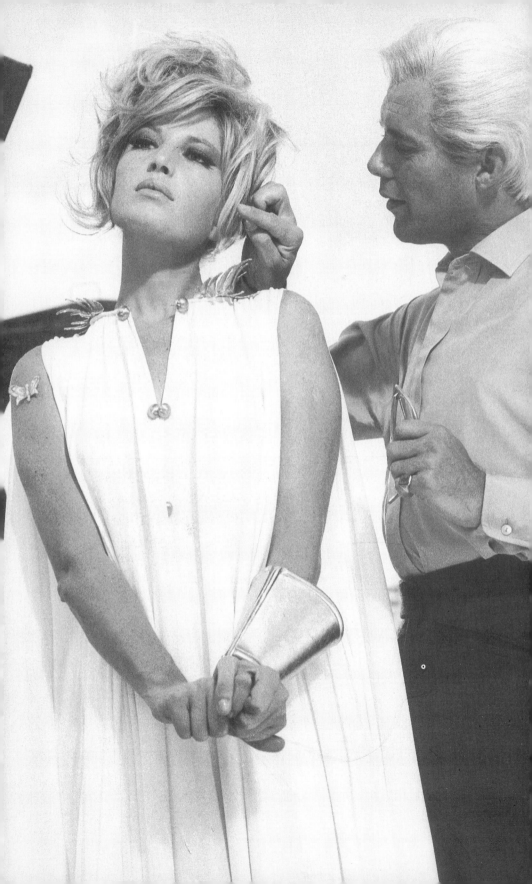

and more sex. June is a humble secretary but Bates has a more elevated position. He whiles away the hours sitting at a drawing board and drooling over a girlie mag – full of partly clad nudes, but he acts as if it's really filthy, as do the other lads in the office who try and sneak a peep for themselves. At other times during the working day, he might be scratching his girlfriend's name on his drawing board or wrestling with a colleague on the floor.

For a twenty-five-year-old, he's unnaturally nervous when walking the girlfriend home – in broad daylight and not even a kiss at the front door. The prospect of a date in the cinema is enough to send him hopping away down the street as happy as a sandboy. June, who looks a good deal younger than Bates, acts in a far more mature manner. Why Schlesinger didn't use teenagers is a bit of a mystery – until one remembers that none of the kids in the Cliff Richard musical *The Young Ones* was under twenty with a couple pushing thirty.

After holding hands in the circle, our ageing 'teenage' couple graduate to a kiss and a cuddle in the park and a good grope on the river bank which freaks them out. Bates goes back to the boys until June talks him into having another try. Cut to a chemist's shop where Bates, fast approaching middle age, is plucking up courage to buy a condom. Instead he comes out with a bottle of Lucozade, which obviously doesn't work because June gets pregnant. The 'love scene' is staged with utmost discretion in Mum's front room while she is away for a weekend. June sits demurely naked on the settee while Bates stands at the far end of the room, fully clothed with nothing hanging out but his tie.

No wonder the marriage, when it finally happens, is a disaster. In fairness, this is mainly due to a possessive Mum whose house the couple have to share – an impossible situation which is only resolved when the newlyweds find a place of their own. Maybe this sort of wishy-washy stuff was OK in its day but if it turned up now in an episode of 'Coronation Street' or 'East Enders' the TV would be switched off very quickly!

John's second effort, *Billy Liar* exhibited some of the flair he had dazzled us with on 'Monitor', and I doubt if anyone could have handled the subject better than he. But why he chose it in the first place is a mystery.

It's all about a boy called Billy, played by Tom Courtenay, who dreams of becoming a scriptwriter, while working in a funeral parlour and living at home with his parents somewhere in the sombre Midlands. He escapes from grim reality by dwelling in a land of dreams called Ambrosia, where he is the dictator. But the world he creates is even more sterile than his real world. All he seems to do is dress up as Field Marshal Rommel, make silly speeches at rallies and inspect his troops. He also wields an imaginary machine gun to mow down people who cross him. He dreams of going to bed with one of his girlfriends and nearly goes to London to seek fame and fortune with the other, only to chicken out at the last moment. We last see him marching back home at the head of his army which we know will vanish the moment he enters the front door – to say 'goodnight' to his parents and brush his teeth before going to bed and jerking off. Are we to sympathise with this wanker? If his writing is as barren as his imagination, he has no talent anyway. All he seems to do is upset friends and foes alike. To put it bluntly, Billy is one big pain in the ass.

Maybe *Billy Liar* seemed a good idea on paper? Maybe it was meant to be a portrait of a schizophrenic? Who knows? Certainly any healthy male who turns down an opportunity to run off to London with the young Julie Christie must be off his chump.

John discovered Julie Christie. She first appeared, I believe, in a film he made for 'Monitor' called *Hi-Fi-Fo-Fum*, a brilliant satire on the High Fidelity revolution that was sweeping England in the late Fifties. Johnny Dankworth and his boys also featured in the same documentary, which I seem to remember was photographed by Ken Higgens, a talented BBC cameraman. These same artists made notable contributions to John's next feature film, *Darling*.

The fact that it now appears dated is a point in its favour. As a portrait of a swinger in the Swinging Sixties it is unique. Shallow relationships, bloated egos and cold-blooded betrayals are the order of the day in Frederic Raphael's tale of a shallow trendy of her times – Diana, played by Julie Christie. Her one and only claim to fame is that she is the face of the Sixties, as we see during the opening credits when a giant hoarding of starving Ethiopians is gradually obliterated by a high fashion poster of Diana.

Dirk Bogarde – a roaming BBC reporter – stops her for a vox pop interview in the King's Road, and before you know it they are in bed together, deceiving their respective spouses, or is it 'spices'? Julie Christie sleeps around to further her career, from model to hostess to starlet to Princess – Princess Diana, if you can believe it. On the way *Darling* provides an A–Z of what fashionable, fun couples did at the time – such as booking into an hotel for an afternoon's illicit sex with a suitcase full of newspapers, skimming stones at Chelsea Reach, having an abortion, stealing food from Fortnum and Mason, joining an orgy, smoking pot, drowning your pet goldfish in gin and tonic and throwing it off Hammersmith Bridge in a matchbox. This was the sort of thing that trendy French directors had been making their mistresses do a decade earlier. So who wasn't influenced by the New Wave?

VIII

Far From The Maddening Crowd

It was only natural, after years of photographing the landscapes of London, that my first documentary for 'Monitor' should be about London – John Betjeman's London, to be precise, with the poet himself declaiming his nostalgic verse on subjects as diverse as snow falling in Fenchurch Street Station and business girls taking baths in Camden Town. As this modest fifteen-minute item went down well with the TV viewers, I was allowed to stay on and encouraged to push the conventional documentary format into the unexplored territory of the kaleidoscopic biopic. The subjects I produced over the next decade or so reflected my personal enthusiasms, which were mainly musical. Out of this was born a new enthusiasm – for the British countryside. I'd loved the New Forest since childhood, but that was almost as familiar as my back garden. While filming *Elgar* in the Malvern Hills I was over-whelmingly aware how the sweep and grandeur of the landscape was echoed resoundingly in the composer's music. Older viewers may recall the image of a boy on a white horse galloping over the hills as an evocation of the spirit of delight Elgar sought after.

Many years later a very different vision of the English landscape appeared in Bruce Robinson's second feature film, *How to get ahead in Advertising*. The sequence was not dissimilar to the one in *Elgar*. But Robinson replaces the innocent boy with a corrupt advertising executive whose attitude towards the public he bamboozles with his phoney campaigns is as putrescent as the boil on the side of his neck. This boil gradually swallows up his schizo-phrenic head and takes over. With coat-tails flying like Beelzebub on a jet-black steed, Richard E. Grant is the very spirit of negation. When he reaches the peak of the hill at sunset to survey his kingdom below, it is not with Elgar's tremendous optimism that the lad on the white horse symbolised, but with a gloating contempt for his pathetic brainwashed subjects. A very powerful statement, and a very pessimistic one. I understand that Bruce is working in America now, so I guess he sees little hope for the future here. Let's hope he's wrong.

The countryside of Britain has not fared well on the screen. Apart from a few documentaries in the Thirties it has been comparatively underexposed, until recent times when there has been something of a renaissance. With the example of the success at the box office of American movies about the great outdoors it is odd that it took us so long to take a leaf from Hollywood's book. Apart from all those Westerns, just think of musicals like *Oklahoma* – 'O-kla-ho-ma, where the wind comes sweepin' 'cross the plain.' Perhaps 'Out-er-Orkney, where the wind comes driving in the rain' doesn't have quite the same popular appeal.

But if we haven't made the equivalent of *Oklahoma* over here, we once produced something that equalled it in breezy panache. As usual, Michael Powell was the innovator. What he did for ballet in *The Red Shoes* he did for Shropshire in *Gone to Earth*, the famous novel by Mary Webb. Ironically, the film seems to have been born of California, for surely Hollywood was behind the idea of casting Jennifer Jones as Hazel, a Welsh witch. Whatever the case, it works. Her performance is red in tooth and claw. Jungle drums throb and the wind howls as Hazel, clutching her book of spells, runs barefoot through the bracken to the cottage she shares with her fox, her crow and her father – who is nonchalantly plucking chickens and a Welsh harp. They make an odd couple, the wild girl of the hills and the cantankerous old man, but they're a great team as she sings and he plays at an open-air religious service, conducted by the local minister.

Despite the fact that her mother was a gypsy and dogs whimper when she enters a room, Hazel is a good, hymn-singing girl, or so the minister thinks. Caught in her spell, he proposes marriage and, encouraged by her father, Hazel accepts.

Cut to a country fair, a tumultuous scene of rural life with all its vigour and exuberance spotlit through gaps in summer clouds that drift over the soft, surrounding hills. We have a Punch and Judy show, point-to-point racing, plenty of booze, roundabouts, fortune-tellers, traction engines and a dashing squire, played by David Farrar, who, catching sight of Hazel for the first time, gallops after her through the crowd. How the tongues of the busybodies waggle. 'First the parson, now the squire. It'll be the king on his throne next.'

It is clear that there is a powerful alchemy at work between Hazel and the squire but, sad to say, she has been promised to the parson. So into the church she sails in a stunning bridal gown trailing Foxy on a lead. The simple ceremony is followed with a baptism by total immersion, as the congregation gape at Hazel's nubile body tantalisingly revealed through her clinging wet dress. But the minister has a potency problem and the marriage is not con-summated, so Hazel starts hankering after the squire, who sends her a note suggesting a nocturnal assignation at the local spinney.

Torn between her marriage vows and her natural inclinations, she climbs God's Little Mountain at dusk to seek the answer to her dilemma. Once at the summit, a spooky place of weird white stones, she throws her shawl over the Devil's Chair and utters a prayer. 'If I be meant to go to local spinney, let me hear the fairy music.'

And sure enough she does, filtering up through the evening mists from the valley below. It is Dad playing his harp, deep in a pine forest – but that is good enough for Hazel. Soon a shadow is creeping up her white dress as the squire approaches in the moonlight, trampling underfoot the red roses that have spilled from her bouquet. The next moment they are mounted and riding into the night. More striking images follow, as Hazel wanders barefoot at dawn in a red dress through the squire's magic garden –past watching statues, over a romantic bridge and through a gigantic topiary swan. But it can't last – master and mistress are too similar in temperament – and soon the sparks begin to fly. When the parson turns up to claim his truant bride, she is ready to go home with him. 'You can have her, minister,' shouts the squire, 'When I call her, she'll come running.'

Back in the minister's house, all is chaos. Mum threatens to pack her bags if the scarlet woman stays. Hazel stays, Mum departs, and the minister grows more horny every minute. 'The Lord says the adulteress must go,' pronounces a deputation of local worthies. The adulteress goes – to save Foxy who can't stand the humbug of the humans a minute longer and has bolted through the doorway to freedom.

Bad timing. The local hunt is riding to hounds. Soon the sound of braying dogs tells us they have picked up Foxy's scent. Then Hazel grabs poor, exhausted Foxy in her arms and runs like hell. Marvellous shots of the chase, involving the minister, the squire, Hazel, Foxy and the frenzied hounds tearing through the purple heather. Suddenly it's over. 'Gone to earth' echoes mournfully around the hills, as dark thunderclouds gather over the abandoned mineshaft down which the two hunted creatures have found refuge in death.

Novelettish? Not in the hands of Michael Powell. Christopher Challis's photography sparkles like a Constable and resonates like the Pastoral Symphony of Vaughan Williams. Pity that Powell didn't use V.W. instead of his composer-in-residence, Brian Easdale, whose throbbing tom-toms were put to better use in *Black Narcissus*, another film starring David Farrar which I mention here because most of the exteriors were also filmed on the Welsh borders.

But instead of spells and witchery, with *Black Narcissus* we have prayers and good works, and a band of nuns taking over an old harem in Tibet where they have been sent to save the heathen. This they do by administering large doses of French and castor oil, a combination which brings about at least one fatality. Meanwhile busty houris smile voluptuously down from faded murals as if remembering past pleasures, while their chaste sisters only go down on their knees to pray. What more potent symbol for the external war between flesh and the spirit? And that's what the film is all about. So, as wind machines whirr through the big open windows, setting the habits of the nuns swirling, their emotions begin to do likewise with the arrival on their doorstep of a handsome Englishman gone to seed. Sporting a baggy pair of shorts and a big straw hat, he turns up for Christmas carols, a little more merry than the occasion demands.

The sight of the goose pimples on his bare, bony knees, while incurring the wrath of the Mother Superior, drives one of the sex-starved sisters completely round the twist. Secretly she sends away to Calcutta for a more seductive, secular outfit. Then, one dark and stormy night, she puts on scarlet lipstick, a scarlet frock, a pair of king-size lambswool flying boots, and sneaks out of the convent, as fast as her footwear will allow, towards the seedy Englishman's bungalow.

Once inside she loses no time in trying to seduce him, but the only thing that gets stiff is his upper lip. Could it be that he is gay? Before the arrival of the nuns the old harem had been occupied for a while by a bevy of monks. Either way, the twisted sister leaves his bungalow and takes out her frustration on the Mother Superior – by trying to push her off the mountain-top as she rings the Angelus. Instead, it is she who goes flying down into the abyss, after tripping over her king-size flying boots.

After that, the nuns admit defeat and go home to Mum, leaving the murals of the smiling houris with the last laugh. All very theatrical, including the sets and painted backdrops of the Himalayas seen through gaping windows. But if the studio work jarred with the naturalism of the exteriors, the excellence of the acting smoothed things over. Deborah Kerr was particularly good, both as the harassed Mother Superior and as the victim of an unhappy love affair during her earlier fox-hunting days back in Ireland – seen in flashback. Powell's treatment of the theme of sexual obsession was muted in most of his films. When he finally did come out of the closet with *Peeping Tom*, he never worked again – at least not in England. But, if the kinky sex in that mould-breaking masterpiece was right up front, it was certainly not the case either in *Black Narcissus* or in another of Powell's pastoral essays, *A Canterbury Tale*.

Over shots of medieval extras trudging along a cart track, a narrator tells us that for close on a thousand years the Canterbury Way has been a busy road for pilgrims seeking an answer to their prayers. We then see a falconer sending his hawk into the skies where, in a clever cut, it turns into a Spitfire, and we have skipped the intervening centuries to find ourselves in the Kentish country-side towards the end of World War II – a place of army manoeuvres, with Bren-gun carriers, pretty land girls and battalions of US troops waiting for D-Day. The action centres around a picture postcard village full of quaint locals and a village idiot. Could he be the nocturnal nutter responsible for pouring glue on the hair of the local lasses known to fraternise with the troops? No. The guilty culprit turns out to be none other than the local magistrate who reasons that his sticky shampoos will keep the women home at night, leaving the men no alternative but to attend his boring magic lantern lectures on the history of England.

The magistrate's quirky secret only comes to light in the last reel, when he is exposed in a railway carriage by some other leading member of the cast. Will they turn him over to the police when they reach Canterbury or will they not? To be honest, I can't remember. Probably not, for in one way or another they all have their prayers answered. The land girl heroine discovers that the brave boyfriend she thought killed in action is alive and well, while the ex-cinema organist gets to play the cathedral organ as his battalion march up the aisle singing 'Onward Christian Soldiers'.

Was there a deviant streak in Michael Powell? Why take an allegory based on Chaucer's *Canterbury Tales* and inject it with a shot of glutinous perversity? Although, in his defence, Powell's little jab was as nothing compared with the lethal overdose administered by that unmentionable Italian pervert who, not content with killing off Chaucer's classic, committed necrophilia as well.

Powell's film would have been a lot better without the glue-sniffer, though I guess he would have fought tooth and nail to retain it if the distributors had advised him to cut it. I speak from experience. I had a battle with United Artists over *Valentino*. They argued loud and long for me to remove the infamous jail scene, protesting that it was out of key with the rest of the picture. The sequence in question showed an unforgettable night Valentino spent behind bars while being held on a charge of bigamy. When they learn the identity of the latest inmate, the lowlifes who share his cage subject Valentino to a constant stream of abuse, while performing a series of lewd sexual acts. In this they are aided and abetted by a sadistic jailer who has denied Valentino toilet privileges, while putting a little something in his coffee to 'make him wanna piss all night'. The star's subsequent incontinence drives the inmates to heights of almost animal hysteria that literally send Valentino up the wall as he climbs into the corner of his cage in a hopeless bid to escape their inhuman mockery.

Sound a bit over the top? United Artists thought so too, but let me have my own way, nevertheless. The film did not do well on its release but fared better when it hit the US TV networks fifteen years later – minus that controversial scene which was cut by order of the network censor. I was working in the States at the time and watched the transmission with gritted teeth. What d'you know? The film was a million times better without it.

Without the glue-sniffer, Powell's film is a hymn of thanksgiving for the English countryside, on which the sun shines eternal. It's a pity that Alan Grey's celestial choirs sound closer to Hollywood than Canterbury. Fortunately no such accusation can be levelled against Richard Rodney Bennet, who captured the autumnal Wessex land-scapes of *Far From the Madding Crowd* with music of a more indigenous nature. When a sudden gale threatens to destroy an unprotected haystack, the composer whips up a thrilling orchestral storm in the form of a wild folk dance worthy of Vaughan Williams.

John Schlesinger's flirtation with the countryside in this film is not always so harmonious. He even gets off to a bad start, despite the fact that Hardy has written him one of the greatest cinematic openers of all time. In the novel, a horse and cart trundle over the Downs, piled high with furniture. Seated on the top is our winsome heroine, Bathsheba, admiring herself in a dressing-table mirror and looking like a queen. This is the first sight the shepherd boy hero, Gabriel Oak, has of a beauty he has only dreamed of. No wonder he is blown away.

In the Frederic Raphael script we have a long shot of Julie Christie or her double, galloping across the screen like the female lead in any old Western, shouting, if memory serves me right, 'Hi, Gabriel!' Why do scriptwriters always think they can do better than the original author? One of the worst offenders is Harold Pinter who thought he could improve on not one but two classics, F. Scott Fitzgerald's *The Last Tycoon* and John Fowles' *The French Lieutenant's Woman*. Perhaps the commissioning producers are to blame – they often think that they are not getting their money's worth unless everything is rewritten but the title.

On the whole, Raphael did a serviceable job in adapting Hardy's masterpiece, as did Schlesinger as director, though it was difficult to shake off the feeling that they would both have been happier in W1 than Wessex. The same criticism applies to Julie Christie, who acts for most of the film like 'Darling' in a poke bonnet, while Alan Bates as a son of the soil is also out of his depth. What shepherd worth his salt would command his dog to 'Come here'? You only have to watch 'One Man and His Dog' on TV to know that it's all done by piercing whistles and barbaric curses.

The most convincing character in the film is Troy, the no-good glam soldier in scarlet and gold who sweeps Bathsheba off her feet. In a scene that is almost hallucinatory in its impact, Troy swirls his sabre 295 times around Bathsheba's head in a dazzling display of swordsmanship that's all shimmering soft focus and full of danger. Bully for the editor! It is one of the most breathtaking displays of courtship ever seen, exquisitely conceived and executed. We, the audience, feel as bedazzled as Bathsheba herself.

And, if Troy seems less dated than some of the other players, it's precisely because he is the most dated of all with his Sixties hairdo and gay hussar's uniform – available at the time on any old clothes stall in any metropolitan street market.

Another haunting image is the cart bearing a coffin, passing through a forest after a recent storm, where the only mourners for the forgotten workhouse girl are the aged trees who remember her as a child and weep on her coffin. Here's another marvellous scene – Bathsheba telling Troy of her love for him on Weymouth beach, as a military band and the Atlantic breakers drown out the words which are falling on deaf ears.

Superb production design by Richard MacDonald, a native of those parts, plus Nic Roeg's photography, did Hardy's Wessex (or Dorset) proud, as did the local extras who played an important part in the action.

Britain's seaside resorts suit Panavision screens rather well, and it's a wonder we don't see them more frequently. Brighton looked bright and breezy in *Half a Sixpence*, with Tommy Steele dancing among the beach huts with a lot of Edwardian bathing belles. More recently, Clacton came into its own with the phrase that has backed many a saucy seaside postcard for over a century – *Wish You Were Here*.

Here we had broad humour to match catchphrases like 'Up your bum', as when a condom is dragged from under the bed by a dog at a compromising moment. There's also plenty of sex in this romp of a film about an adolescent losing her cherry in a small seaside town, where the most exciting thing in the place is – herself. She's a bit of a rebel without much of a cause, and something of a snob when it comes to bringing her guns to bear on the enemy.

One target of displeasure is the genteel tearoom where she works, and its harmless habitués. To me one of the few remaining glories of the typical English seaside resort is the 'Tudor Tearoom', or it could be the 'Honeypot', 'Cosy Corner' or 'Bide a While'. Best of all is the Palm Court of the Grand Hotel, with waitresses in smart black uniforms and white lace trimmings. There is much talk about the wonders of the Japanese tea ceremony but precious little about that eighth wonder of the world – the Great British Afternoon Tea. That's a ceremony if ever there was one. My God, it's almost a religion. It's certainly a form of art, but a dying art, alas, if the barbarians have their way. Darjeeling, Ceylon, Lapsang Souchong, Indian, Earl Grey, with lemon, or milk, milk in first? sugar? how many lumps? a scrambled egg and watercress sandwich? or would you prefer cucumber, or smoked salmon, or muffins or teacakes, or a nice piece of crumpet – now, now! – or scones with strawberry preserve and cream? Ah, here comes the cake trolley, gliding through the columned hall, pushed by the ghost of John Betjeman, past the string trio playing 'I get a Kick out of You'. Meringues, éclairs, chocolate truffles and iced fancies. Simple pleasures bringing great satisfaction for a modest outlay in relaxing surroundings – all ridiculed and mocked by our very with-it heroine (and her writer/director) who probably prefers plastic to damask cloth, muzak to music, trash food to trifle, and quick, quick to slow, slow, slow. Wham, bam, thank you, ma'am! Glad I'm Not There.

Another glory of the seaside is also disappearing fast, owing to the indifference of local councils who see their beautiful piers as so much lucrative scrap metal going to waste. How can these monuments to past pleasures be expected to pay their way if they are simply allowed to rot and rust away? What we need is someone with imagination to transform them into places where people want to be, as they did not so long ago. Sounds like an idea for a film, doesn't it?

Yes, and the film was called *All At Sea*, by Charles Frend. And yes, it's yet another Ealing comedy on a disappearing English institution. It occurs to me that perhaps the time is ripe for a comedy on another great English institution that outlived its day – Ealing Films themselves. I hear the BBC have just sold the studios. What will take its place – another supermarket, as was the case with Elstree? One thing's for sure – it's another nail in the coffin of British films.

Back to the Charles Frend caper, with a hairy Alec Guinness playing a thick, ancient Brit in furs paddling a coracle in ever-decreasing circles. 'From the dawn of history,' a voice intones on the soundtrack, 'we have always moved in nautical circles.' After following generations of Guinness, the seafaring man, through the dissolving pages of history we find him ending his days as a captain (R.N. Retired) in command of a pier – the perfect haven for a mariner with a passion for the sea but prone to *mal de mer*. He loves his pier so much that he lives there – in a crazy house with sloping floors and a distorting mirror, in which we catch him shaving. But he's living in a fool's paradise, as he finds out when the local council serves him a compulsory purchase order. However, their plans to line their own pockets in redeveloping the site are neatly thwarted when Guinness removes six feet of planking – thus separating the pier from the mainland – and registers it as a ship. No way can a council requisition a ship. Guinness proceeds to convert his new vessel into a cruise liner that never puts to sea – until the baddies bring up a dredger under cover of darkness to undermine the supports. Then Guinness and his gallant crew stage a counterattack in pedalos and the dredger is repulsed. By this time I was dozing and can't quite remember what happened next, though I do have a picture in my mind's eye of Guinness back on the bridge of his pier drifting majestically across the moonlit channel to France.

Not a bad idea, but Guinness and his pier did not have the pulling power of, say, *Those Magnificent Men in their Flying Machines* and the film did not do well at the box office. Neither did another seaside comedy in which a pier played a very important part – *French Dressing*. Like oil and vinegar, the ingredients didn't mix. A script by a couple of West End review writers didn't jell with the images concocted by an arty director from TV making his first feature. The story, such as it was, concerned the efforts of two lowly council workers to entice a glamorous French film star to their run-down resort in order to inaugurate a film festival and a nudist beach. Despite the efforts of the mayor and corporation to screw things up, the two council workers more or less succeed. Yes, it's that tired old cliché about bad boys on the council knocking a new idea on the head, then cashing in on it when it pays off, thanks to the ingenuity of others.

Where would our comedies be without our crooked mayors and killjoy councillors? Our poor heroes, Roy Kinnear and James Booth, as the Entertainments Officer and Chief Deck Chair Attendant, are saddled with lousy dialogue and a director who seems more concerned with composition than content. There are a few visual gags, mostly at the expense of the mayor and corporation, but there's only so much comedy you can wring out of extras in top hats and tails making fools of themselves on a beach with buckets and spades and Hula-Hoops. One of the best moments comes when the dais, from which the wretched mayor and his corporation are watching a pathetic carnival procession, gets a knock which sends it down a slipway into the sea. In reality everyone would have jumped off before it hit the water but the director insisted that everyone should remain firmly in their seats until the whole edifice is drifting out to sea, at which point they all strike out for the shore singing 'Rule Britannia'. Ludicrous! I actually heard the director compare his film with Jacques Tati's *Monsieur Hulot's Holiday*. What arrogance! Dream on, Mr Director, dream on. The only truly French touch in your flop of a film came from the pen of Georges Delerue. Undoubtedly, the scintillating score – Georges' first ever outside his native France – was the best thing in the movie.

Sometime in the mid-Sixties I made a documentary on this great film composer for the 'Monitor' programme and found him a most accommodating man, brimming with ideas and enthusiasm. I was overjoyed, a couple of years later, when he agreed to write the score for *Women in Love*. When he saw the cut of the film he was overwhelmed. He wasn't the only one. People still come up to me in the street and say it changed their lives. Complete strangers at film festivals stop me and say 'I'm a great fan of yours, and I simply love . . .' (you wait for it, hoping against hope that it will be your last movie they are about to extol but no, it's always) '. . . *Women in Love*.' I nod and smile, but maybe I should react like that superb jazz trumpeter, Miles Davis, who always replied to unsought opinions, from friends and foes, with a cryptic 'So what?'

We all love to be loved, but, when love is blind, it gets a bit wearing. I've made better films than *Women in Love* but obviously it had something that tickled the public's fancy, and it wasn't just the male members of Messrs Bates and Reed. It might have probed intimacy between the sexes as few movies had before, but I can take scant credit for that. I was only putting on the screen what D.H. Lawrence had written half a century before. But the film did have some excellent performances – Glenda won an Oscar – and both Alan and Olly really came to grips with the subject, especially in the nude wrestling scene.

I wonder if people would still be talking about the film today if I hadn't included that particular sequence . . . It wasn't in the original script. I didn't think it would pass the censor and I knew it would be difficult to shoot. I was wrong on my first guess and right on my second. Olly talked me into it. He wrestled with me, jujitsu style, in my kitchen, and wouldn't let me up until I said, 'OK, OK, you win, I'll do it.' Hell! I was in pain. Thanks, Olly, we made history.

But it's impossible to film a 600-page novel and be true to the author's vision. Two hours is about all anyone can take at a sitting. Many great scenes had to be sacrificed. I particularly regret the omission of the Brangwen girls' sojourn in London where they sample *la vie bohème*. It helped form their characters and explains their subsequent behaviour. And at least two of the actors were miscast. Another had to be replaced after his second appearance. But none of that matters when a movie turns you on. You can have brilliant camerawork, great editing, a fine script and good acting, but it don't mean a thing if it ain't got that swing.

We broached this subject by way of music, which brings us back to Georges Delerue, who had such a high regard for the film that he made the mistake of trying to write an orchestral masterpiece. It was inappropriate and I had to drop it. Yet Georges had turned in such a brilliant score for *French Dressing*, which needed all the help it could get. There were no restraints there; he could just let himself go. His best moment in *Women in Love* came with the waltz he composed for the naked lovers floating up to heaven in clouds of pink flowers – the schmaltziest moment in the film that would have made Lawrence turn in his grave had his wife, Frieda, not thoughtfully buried his ashes in a ton of concrete. I hope Georges, another genius who died in a foreign country, was more fortunate.

IX

Made In Britain

I had no such musical headaches in my next film, *The Music Lovers*. How could I, when Tchaikovsky was the subject? I'd already formulated my approach to the genre in films for 'Monitor' on Prokofiev, Elgar, Bartok, Debussy and Richard Strauss. My intention was never to produce a factual, day-by-day account of the composer's life – that's the stuff of newsreels, explaining nothing of the man's inner life. What I've always been after is the spirit of the composer as manifest in his music. This cannot be expressed in either a straightforward, dramatised documentary or in a fictionalised feature film. I try to achieve the cinematic equivalent of a musical form such as Tchaikovsky's Theme and Variations from Suite No. 3 in G.

The theme of *The Music Lovers* was 'love' itself and the variations were the various forms it played in Tchaikovsky's life and music. He experienced the romantic, the incestuous, the homosexual and the maternal, and they all found expression in his music.

Passion in British films worries some people. I suppose that is why there's not so much of it about. God freaks them out too, which is why we make so few films with religious themes. Apart from *The Cardinal* and *The Devils*, I can't think of any. Neither have we made a feature film on a composer worth seeing, apart from *The Music Lovers, Mahler* and Tony Palmer's *Testimony*, based on the life of Shostakovich. But Palmer comes from TV, where musical biopics are the norm – and that's where we have to look these days for our mass cultural sustenance. And when the small screen in the living room has expanded to the size of the wall (as it will by the end of the decade), then it will be curtains for the cinema.

So, if we are weak on religion and art, what is the strength of the British feature film? What are we best known for abroad? I suppose it's the Bond films.

As we all know, violence on the screen, for most censors in the world, is deemed preferable to sex, especially where children are concerned. And, although most kids would have no difficulty in describing in graphic detail how the baddies meet their end in any given Bond film, they'd be hard pressed to remember anything of excitement happening beneath the sheets – unless of course it's a hairy tarantula going down on Mr Bond in *Dr No.* Instead of the real thing we get heavy innuendo.

Some of the films in this interminable series seem to be aimed specifically at the under-tens, the prime example being *Octopussy.* This was real *Boys' Own Paper* stuff – with fist-fights on the wings of speeding aircraft, chases along the tops of trains, circus clowns shot from cannons, and James Bond swinging through the trees bellowing like Tarzan above crocodile-infested waters, where one of the reptiles turns out to be a midget submarine and the villain hides nearby playing with a yo-yo in the shape of a circular saw.

But there is something for Dad, too, in the form of a philanthropic queen of the jungle, and the nubile handmaidens she has saved from the streets to train as a troupe of circus acrobats – who come in handy when, along with 007, they raid the baddies' HQ. The plot can be summed up in one sentence. Manic Russian General tries to detonate an atomic bomb during a circus act at an American air base in Germany so that it will look like an accident for which the Yanks will be held responsible. The maniac is foiled – but with only seconds to spare.

This particular Bond was a cut-price affair, the most costly prop being a galleon, (wo)manned by fifty whores all pulling on their oars. As the ship glides serenely through the water, we cut below deck to find 007 hard at it with Octopussy herself, as the cox shouts 'In, out; in, out; in, out'! – which probably makes this cheap laugh the most expensive joke in motion picture history. How Gerald Thomas let that gag get away from *Carry on, Cleo* is a mystery.

Despite the fact that the Bond films have had even more directors working on the series than actors portraying 007, there is a remarkable consistency of style – with one or two noteworthy exceptions. *A View to a Kill* comes pretty high on the list in that respect, with Bond making his first appearance in Gucci ski wear – a proper pouf, according to a patron sitting next to me at my local fleapit. Pouf or not, he does some spectacular stunts on skis for the first reel or so – or at least his double does – including some fancy footwork on just one ski as he leads his pursuers a merry chase over the Alps, and across a thawing lake of ice in which most of them drown as he jumps to safety on a mini-iceberg which turns out to be yet another one-man submarine.

Needless to say, it is piloted by a woman as nicely upholstered as the divan on which James collapses. More amusing stunts follow, with a spectacular jump from the Eiffel Tower to a *bateau-mouche*. On to an elegant château, with Vivaldi and caviare, elegant partygoers and thoroughbred horses. But the ghost of Gerald Thomas, like Felix, keeps on walking and it is not long before we are back in *Carry on* territory. Sitting in a jacuzzi massaging a beautiful Russian spy James asks, 'Would you like it a little harder?' To which the BRS replies, as *Swan Lake* plays on the stereo, 'You're tickling my . . . Tchaikovsky.'

However, this particular Bond saw a breakthrough with a woman (after twenty years or so) finally getting on top, in bed. But when one remembers that the woman was Grace Jones, the innovation seems inevitable.

Bond was a bonanza at the box office in the early days, but, as the grosses diminished, so did the budgets that paid for all the gadgets and gizmos that were a crucial part of the fun. The only device of interest in *Live and Let Die* is the magnetic watch Bond uses to unzip a girl's dress. Later we are reduced to really low-budget stuff, when, to destroy a deadly snake, James is forced to use a can of aftershave and a cigarette lighter. Later still, we degenerate to old-fashioned fisticuffs, hang-gliders and gypsy fortune-tellers. And, although Bond ends up in bed with Jane Seymour, even less happens than usual.

But why go on?

Bond made many people rich, including John Barry, who nearly always provided the music. The famous 007 theme may even outlive the character who inspired it. Harry Saltzman, the co-producer, became a multimillionaire. Having made his fortune from one undercover agent working for HM government, maybe he thought he could double it by producing another. The result was a trilogy featuring Harry Palmer – a one-time private eye pressed into working for the Special Branch against his will. Whereas the brainchild of Ian Fleming was born with a silver spoon in his mouth, Len Deighton's offspring grew up within the sound of Bow Bells. Where Bond gets by on acrobatics and gadgetry, Palmer uses cockney guile. But when it comes to it, they can both use their fists and both have a way with the ladies. Bond is sophisticated and has a good nose for a wine whereas Palmer couldn't tell a *Bitte* from a lager. Bond says it with flowers, Palmer says it with his bedroom eyes. And they both get into trouble the moment they get into bed. In fact, the more one analyses them, the more similar they become – different sides of the same coin. Yet of the two, the rich man fared better at the box office than the poor man. Hi-tech triumphed over tenacity as is proven by their respective track records.

So far there have been more Bond films than Bond books, against only three featuring Harry Palmer – *The Ipcress File, Funeral in*

Berlin and finally *Billion Dollar Brain*. The last, according to Anne Billson, was the best of the bunch.

'The story is confusing certainly, but served up with a panache that was nowhere to be seen in the equally confusing *Funeral in Berlin* . . . but Russell's cinematic flair, for some reason, tends to upset critics, who seem to regard it as unsporting, even un-British. The plot is years ahead of its time, anticipating glasnost in its teaming of East and West, united against a common foe, in this case a Texan millionaire whose rabid anti-communism seems set to trigger off World War III. When he realises what the Texan is up to, Palmer pools his resources with his old chum Colonel Stok (of the KGB) and the film climaxes with the forces of anti-communism drowning in the Baltic as the ice cracks around them – homage to the battle on the ice at the end of Sergei Eisenstein's *Alexander Nevsky*.

'Most of the film was shot in Finland where Russell and his cinematographer, Billy Williams, exploit every last variation of the photogenic possibilities of the snow-covered landscapes and steel-grey skies. What *Billion Dollar Brain* has, which the first two Harry Palmer films lack, is a dreamlike quality which lingers in the memory long after films with more meretricious plotting have faded.'

Rumour has it that Michael Caine encouraged Harry Saltzman to give me a try after seeing one of my 'Monitor' programmes. It might have been the Debussy film with a highly original script by Melvyn Bragg. When Harold Pinter used a similar device twenty-odd years later, everyone said, 'How innovative!'

We were given plenty of room to experiment on 'Monitor' and I found that alternating between the small screen and the big one kept me gainfully employed all the year round. Big screen, small screen, square or oblong, what's the difference – all films end up on the small screen eventually. Those were the days when the world was my oyster. Whether the films were made for viewing in the cinema or at home, they were all about subjects dear to my heart. From the mid-Sixties and for many years after, I was given carte blanche to make whatever I wanted, both by the BBC and big American distributors like United Artists, Warner Brothers and MGM. Big oaks from little acorns grow.

X

The Northern New Wave

My little acorn came in the shape of a clockwork camera I used to borrow to shoot my amateur movies. I wonder what became of it?

It was a 16 mm Paillard Bolex, belonging to a documentary company in Soho Square. From Monday to Friday they put it to regular use but at weekends it often became available – thanks, I seem to remember, to the philanthropy of one of the more lowly members of the staff who lent it gratis to the likes of me. Well, not quite 'the likes' perhaps, because the other enthusiastic amateurs in the queue were Karel Reisz, Lindsay Anderson and Tony Richardson.

Although I never came into contact with them individually until many years later, the other three aspiring directors probably knew each other well, for they shared similar interests, which resulted in documentaries like 'We are the Lambeth Boys', 'O Dreamland' (Margate funfair) and 'Every Day Except Christmas' (Covent Garden market). These young cineastes were part of a group known as Free Cinema – presumably because they received free handouts from the British Film Institute. But whereas their approach was rooted in the wartime documentaries of Humphrey Jennings, I was inspired by the bold imagery of Fritz Lang and the surreal world of Jean Cocteau.

Lourdes was my first film in colour. It had no synch dialogue and, for the most part, relied on quotes from the Blessed Virgin Mary to tell the story, with Benjamin Britten's vivid music backing up my view of that disturbing Catholic shrine. I was director, writer and cameraman – a sort of Father, Son and Holy Ghost. Huw Wheldon was too busy to see *Lourdes* and, in retrospect, I think it was just as well, for, being a Welsh Presbyterian, he might have found it to be one Catholic film of mine too many. He had given me that much sought-after job with 'Monitor' on the strength of *Amelia and the Angel*.

That film was made with all the zeal of a new convert burning to affirm his faith. The story was simplicity itself, and followed the adventures of a Catholic schoolgirl who disobeys her teacher and takes home the angel wings she will be wearing in a nativity play. The wings get broken beyond repair, and our little heroine gives way to tears and despair. But it is only a momentary lapse. Amelia pulls herself together and prays to her patron saint and guardian angel to help her find a new pair of wings before nightfall. Between them they manage to pull off a miracle just as the sun is setting over Kensington Gardens.

The film is not as yukky as it sounds, mainly due to its little star – a ten-year-old Argentinian angel, called Mercedes Quadros. The remainder of the cast included most of my neighbours in the tumbledown boarding house where I was living at the time. As with *Lourdes*, *Amelia* had a compelling music track and (to remind you) no synch dialogue. That's mostly how I told my story – with pictures and music, plus minimal narration.

Everything I have made since owes a lot to the style of those two amateur films, and I have spent some time on them because it helps define my general attitude towards the cinema. I sometimes think I would fare better in the hands of British critics if I was called Russellini. They may forgive Fellini his excesses, but I am chastised for being theatrical, although until recently I had not worked on the stage, whereas Lindsay Anderson and Tony Richardson have divided their talents more or less equally between the two, from the very start of their careers.

One of Tony's early features started life as a play which he produced at the Royal Court Theatre in Sloane Square, where it created something of a sensation. It was called *A Taste of Honey* and was written by Shelagh Delaney, a young girl from Salford. I made a documentary on her for 'Monitor' to coincide with the première of her second play, *The Lion in Love*, which unfortunately did not enjoy the same success. *A Taste of Honey* told the age-old story of a young girl's coming of age and was partly autobiographical. When I did my film on Shelagh, Salford was a slum of crumbling back-to-backs, a graveyard of young hopes. All Shelagh wanted to do was get out, before it killed her. The heroine of her play felt much the same. This was tailor-made for Tony. The result was a touching portrayal of a wide-eyed schoolgirl who runs away from Mum, lives with a homosexual, gets pregnant by a black man and goes back to Mum. Not an earth-shattering story, perhaps, but with Rita Tushingham making her screen debut as the teenage heroine, Tony could hardly go wrong. Unlike some other members of the English Northern New Wave, the heroine was sympathetic for once, but more of that later . . .

After that brilliant start, Tony continued to produce an impressive body of work, both on stage and screen. *Look Back in Anger* and *The Entertainer* were the most noteworthy. Tony was so prolific he was difficult to keep up with. One day, long before I had established myself as a features director, he invited me to his office at Woodfall Films in Mayfair and asked if I'd be interested in making a film starring his wife, Vanessa Redgrave. His company owned a novel called *Seven Lean Years*, about a young woman going to seed in a run-down Victorian rooming house in West London. He'd seen a dramatised documentary I'd made for the BBC film unit on a similar subject called 'A House in Bayswater' and he commissioned me to write a script. He too was working on a screenplay, and I'm pretty sure it was *Tom Jones*. You will find no mention of my little script in the annals of British screen history, whereas Tony's screenplay of Fielding's eighteenth-century romp turned out to be something of a break-through.

Historically, it wasn't far removed from the world of *The Wicked Lady*, but, when a highwayman in Tony's film shouted 'Stand and deliver!', he didn't get a handful of jewels in reply but a gutsy 'What do you think I am, a travelling midwife?'

Whereas Gainsborough Films were shot in black and white on overlit studio sets, where the camera was nailed to the floor and the outdoors was invariably indoors, Tony used fast colour stock, available light, real stately homes and a camera that was more at home in the air than on the ground. Amendment! For Tony, read Walter, the director of photography – Walter Lassally, who was responsible for some of the best cinematography in the Free Cinema series. The point here is that collaboration between director and cinematographer suited to perfection the freewheeling style of the narrative, which is all about true love, mistaken identity and the triumph of good over bad – the bad being a creepy cousin who tries to cheat Tom out of his rightful inheritance. Albert Finney in the lead gave a sparkling performance that made a star of him overnight, and the rest of the cast, including Dame Edith Evans, David Warner and Susannah York, were hardly less good. The film pulsates with energy which reaches its climax in a fantastic hunt scene. Thundering hoofs, thrashing whips, falling bodies, gouging spurs, panting hounds, fleeing deer – shot alternately from a bird's eye view and a worm's eye – and all intercut with a pounding soundtrack that has you on the edge of your saddle.

And who can ever forget the great eating scene between the eager Tom and that bitch on heat, Mrs Waters, as they face each other across the dining table, devouring each other with lust as they savour, sniff and swallow course after course – oysters, pheasants, lobsters, licking their lips, sucking their fingers as they eat their way faster and faster towards the four-poster and just deserts.

That's what I thought at the time, but the film has not worn well. When I saw it again recently, I noticed an air of desperation in the way the hand-held camera panned relentlessly hither and thither in the hope of catching something of interest, at the same time trying to convince us that the pace is fast and furious. Actually, the film is pretty pedestrian, a fault John Addison's galloping harpsichord tries hard to disguise. Some of the dark goings-on are so dark you can hardly see what's happening. There are also a few too many rural meanderings as the lovers moon and spoon through field and meadow. But we're all rather guilty of that, I'm afraid. I did the same in *The Music Lovers* with Tchaikovsky and his sister drifting through romantic landscapes hand in hand, to the strains of the B Flat Minor Piano Concerto.

Eventually, Tony lost control when attempting to bring Evelyn Waugh's *The Loved One* to the screen. It was too over-the-top for words, but in my view, it is far better to OD than be crippled by restraint.

I rather lost track of Tony's career after *The Loved One*. I know that he fell out with the critics and didn't even bother with a press show for his vastly underrated *The Charge of the Light Brigade*. Perhaps he also fell out with United Artists, who financed it. That's what happened to me after *Valentino*, which was also a flop. I didn't work again in features for years after that.

And now Tony is dead, gone up to that big cinema in the sky, watching movies of all those crummy critics who maligned him roasting in a Technicolor hell.

Another hugely talented director, Lindsay Anderson, alas, is also no longer with us – as a force in the feature film world, that is. There was a time when he was held in high esteem by the BFI (British Film Inquisition) but that probably did more harm than good in the long run.

Anderson's *This Sporting Life* was an impressive first feature. It was about dirt. Richard Harris, the hero, is first seen, sweaty and

85

grimy, wresting coal from the ground. He is next seen being dragged down in the mud as he fights for the ball in an amateur rugger match. When he turns professional he is treated like dirt by the directors of the club, who shamelessly exploit him, while he in turn treats the waiters in a restaurant like dirt, trying to impress the girlfriend with his new-found affluence. The girlfriend, a grim-faced widow who reluctantly takes him in as a lodger, is treated like dirt by the neighbours when he gives her a fur coat. The town itself is a monument to dirt – a place of squalor and neglect – where no one, either self-seekers or honest folk, can win the game of life, which is anything but sporting. Life is as dirty as everything else.

Strong stuff, made all the more compelling by the committed performances, the brooding score by Roberto Gerhard and the dramatic lighting by Denys Coop – held together by a director who knows exactly what he wants and communicates it to cast and crew. Then what's up, Doc? Why don't we care, when, having attempted and failed to win love, our hero tries to buy it and is brought down into the mud yet again by an unfair tackle? The main reason must be the monumental miscasting. With his mascaraed eyes and charismatic presence, Richard Harris is every inch a cut-price Marlon Brando, whom he appears to be impersonating. But, with her tight-lipped, disapproving glare, shapeless figure and scraped-back hair, Rachel Roberts looks old enough to be his mother – and acts like it. I've often pondered on Roberts and the strange hold she seemed to exert over some of our most talented English directors. As young Albert Finney's last fling before marriage in *Saturday Night and Sunday Morning*, she seems equally unalluring and therefore unbelievable. But director Karel Reisz seems as much under her spell as Lindsay Anderson – and John Schlesinger, come to that.

In *Yanks* it's the same old story. Once again, Roberts is a disapproving, dour-faced, long-suffering northerner, unattractive in looks and personality. She casts a blight over every scene in which she appears. Even when she smiles she looks sour. As I was saying, it is difficult to comprehend Harris's obsession for her in *This Sporting Life*. The only time she seems to achieve contentment is when she is polishing her dead husband's boots.

Maybe Rachel Roberts was from the north herself, like most of the writers who turned out screenplays for the Northern New Wave – people like David Storey, Keith Waterhouse and Willis Hall. Maybe they had a say in the casting and felt more comfortable with a real northern lass around? Who knows? In retrospect, most of these New Wave movies were much of a muchness. Life was dreary, the sun never shone. A drink with the lads was usually more desirable than a date with a girl. Most women were dumb and didn't know about birth control. Although there was a deal of kissing and cuddling on canal banks and in park shelters, someone always got pregnant and, after failing to get rid of it by sitting in a hot bath drinking gin, had it terminated in a squalid back-street parlour by a seedy abortionist.

But people grew tired of the bleak formula, audience and directors alike. It is gone and forgotten – killed off by the Beatles and Dick Lester, who, between them, proved that you could come out of a shit heap – smelling of roses.

Some of these directors succeeded in retaining a social conscience, but changed their style and venue. Consider Lindsay Anderson, whose last major epic, *Britannia Hospital*, was made many years after *This Sporting Life*. Like its predecessor, *If . . .*, it used a hierarchical institution as a metaphor for Britain today – uncaring Britain. A seriously injured man is admitted to casualty and allowed to die because the staff are taking a tea break. 'Rule Britannia' plays as a sheet is placed over his corpse. Terrorism and strike chaos follow, with bomb victims having to wait as nurses discuss overtime while tucking into a bacon and egg breakfast.

I remember carrying Ann-Margret, dressed in a silver catsuit, dripping blood, baked beans, cocoa and foaming detergent, into the casualty department of a north London hospital. The nurse looked at Ann-Margret's gashed hand with the thumb nearly hanging off, listened to what I had to say and, suspecting there might be splinters of glass in the wound, ordered an X-ray. She then eased Ann-Margret into a wheelchair and told us to wait for the porter to wheel her into X-ray – as soon as he returned from his tea break. She then busied herself with other patients as the blood flowed and Ann-Margret did her best not to faint. I offered to wheel her to the department myself. No! This was not permitted, only porters were allowed to push wheelchairs. I offered to carry her. No! No! No! After what seemed an eternity, the porter strolled in and pushed the wheelchair through a door, and five yards up the corridor to the X-ray department. Ann-Margret could have bled to death before she finally got those twenty stitches.

In Lindsay's hospital the poor patients are fed on oranges because the kitchen staff are on strike and involved in a meeting called by their union representative to discuss the Queen's visit. She is to inaugurate a new department of surgical science bestowed by the Bonzai Institute of Tokyo. The point under discussion is whether they should serve the Royal Lunch, which is being delivered courtesy of Fortnum's.

They decide such an act would be an insult to their professional pride and refuse to accept delivery. Meanwhile, the Queen herself is finding it difficult to gain admittance to the hospital, because the pickets outside have stopped all traffic through the gates. But finally the protesters allow an ambulance to enter, in the mistaken assumption that it is carrying bomb victims. Actually it contains the Royal Party. They start their tour by meeting the bolshie kitchen staff, who are all dressed up in their best bib and tucker and are arse-kissing like mad.

The Royal Party do their duty and take their leave, passing through the gates in full view of the agitators, who, as an act of disrespect, turn their backs. In doing so, they come face to face

A Taste of Honey

Sammy and Rosie Get Laid, but never hatch into human beings

Above: The Man in Grey.
Melodrama in Black & White

Left: The Wicked Lady

Darling

A Kind of Loving

Gone to Earth

Billy Liar. Portrait of a wanker. Northern New Wave

Right: *How to Get Ahead in Advertising*

Below: Nun's night out in *Black Narcissus*

Overleaf: 'May I have the pleasure?' Valentino teaches Nijinsky to tango

Right: A slice of the 60s. Julie Christie and Terence Stamp in *Far From the Madding Crowd*

Below: A saucy seaside postcard. *Wish You Were Here*

French Dressing or An English Trifle

Ursula Andress in *Dr No*

Rich Man, Poor Man. James Bond *v* Harry Palmer

Below: Billion Dollar Brain

Above: Outmoded Currency

Left: Ann-Margret in *Tommy*

with the riot police who see this as provocative confrontation – and start laying into everyone with their batons, to the strains of 'God Save the Queen'. A 'woman for peace' offers a policeman a flower – he acknowledges the gift by bashing her over the head with his truncheon.

In the new department an experiment is in progress. A modern Dr Frankenstein is creating a new monster – but a power cut ruins the operation, so they cut off the head of a nosey reporter to substitute a fresh brain. The headless corpse of the reporter strangles a passing doctor, and the revolutionaries 'storm the palace' and end up in a lecture theatre. Here Frankenstein, spouting like a modern-day Lenin, reveals a brain floating in aspic which he christens Genesis the being of the future, heralding a new beginning for mankind, with a brain 100,000 times more powerful than yours or mine. 'But in time,' the doctor prophesies to the rapt audience of revolutionaries, 'it will be replaced by a silicone chip 1/8 mm square. Within fifteen years it will be possible to contain *Homo sapiens* in a matchbox.' Turning back to the floating brain, the nutty professor concludes, 'You see the face of the future, now hear the voice.' The brain speaks:

> 'What a piece of work is a man!
> How noble in reason! how infinite in
> faculty! in form, in moving, how
> express and admirable! in action how
> like an angel! in apprehension how
> like a god, how like a god, how like a
> god...'

The needle has got stuck; the new brain is defective . . . Or does it simply have a one-track mind?

XI

Both Sides of the Park

Sociological studies have attracted many native film makers since the advent of World War II. With few exceptions, these movies have dated badly. Whether they were made for purely commercial reasons or from burning conviction seems to have made little difference to their staying power. Out and out comedies such as *The Man in the White Suit* and *I'm All Right, Jack* seem a good deal fresher today than, say, *Room at the Top* or *This Happy Breed*.

David Lean's picture of a lower-middle-class family between the wars is phoney from the second shot in the film to the penultimate shot, the first and last being panning shots across rooftops to and from a house in Clapham where most of the action is supposed to take place. I say 'supposed' because the intervening scenes are all filmed in the studio. Nothing wrong with that, if the film doesn't look as stagey as the Noel Coward play from which it was adapted. Unfortunately it does, including the garden, glimpsed through the dining-room window, where Frank Gibbons, the head of the family, seems to spend most of his time – apparently with little success because we don't see a single flower in the house for two decades – not even a plastic poppy.

Robert Newton plays Frank and, although he doesn't roll his eyes as much as he did as Long John Silver in *Treasure Island*, he is clearly lost without his wooden leg and his parrot. Instead, Celia Johnson, as his long-suffering wife, does the shrieking. Judging by the hard looks Newton gives her, he would prefer acting with the parrot.

There is no warmth between them. The one time Frank does show a little sentiment she rounds on him with 'That's enough of that, now!'

Everything is 'spelt out' for us in this celebration of mediocrity, from the moment a subtitle states that 'This is the story of a London family 1913–1939'. Other printed messages follow with deadly regularity, including 'Wembley Exhibition 1924', 'A Merry Christmas (card) 1925'. Then we have a newspaper headline reading 'General Strike', followed by a few marching extras with banners, a bus covered in barbed wire and another headline reading 'Strike Over'. Then we have a 1928 fashion magazine followed by 'The Broadway Melody', the all-singing, all-talking, all-dancing sensation of 1929. We also have the Depression, which is what I was beginning to suffer myself by then.

This perfunctory cavalcade of history leaves the Gibbons family singularly unmoved. They go on making tea, washing up, pretending to water the garden and sometimes remembering to drop their aitches and sometimes not, for reel after reel. And, if they appear unmoved by national disasters, personal dramas do affect them, such as when their kids get mixed up with socialists or run off with married men to Marseilles. But they weather these storms because they have 'London Pride' (composed by Noel Coward) which swells up on the soundtrack as Mum and Dad finally leave their wretched semi to take up residence in a block of flats to face further horrors in World War II. Thank God we were spared the sequel. This was David Lean's first solo epic. Fortunately, for the majority of cinemagoers, it was not his last.

But if Lean went on to better things, Celia Johnson went from bad to worse, when she sank even lower down the social scale. In *A Kid for Two Farthings* she seems to be a player in search of a part, spending most of her time in Petticoat Lane, hovering uncertainly between an old clothes stall and a poor Jewish tailor's shop run by David Kossoff. Between his schmaltzy Yiddish philosophising and the shabby garments she has to sell in order to keep body and soul together, life is hell. And if she is a little more hoity-toity than the character warrants, we must remember that she is slumming and that her dreamer of a husband has just popped off to Africa to make a fortune and build them a fabulous dream house. This is a film in which everyone dreams of something, from the old Jewish tailor who dreams of acquiring a steam press to the local lovely, played with a pout by Diana Dors, who dreams of getting a wedding ring from her poufy body-building boyfriend, whose hair is even more beautifully permed than her own. Once again, nothing is real except the opening shots of an East End street market where Celia's six-year-old stuck-up boychick stalks a pigeon among the coster-mongers' stalls – and nearly shits himself when it turns round and pecks him. Yet Carol Reed had a reputation for being wonderful with children.

However, the boychick fares better when he comes to grips with a unicorn which the stooping and bespectacled old Jewish tailor tells him will grant his wishes. Well, the boychick thinks his pet is a unicorn because the kid he gets cheap from a passing vagrant has a little horn just off centre in its forehead which everyone else knows has been stuck on by the prop-man. Nevertheless, we can guess from the sentimental score by Ben Frankel that everyone will achieve their heart's desire and, of course, they do.

The story is so sickly, it's a wonder Steven Spielberg hasn't shot a remake with Richard Dreyfuss playing the old Jewish tailor. It had one good line (and one only) that he'd probably appreciate, which is cracked by a younger, more successful Jewish tailor played by Sydney Tafler. 'You've heard of Christian Dior,' he shouts to the passing shoppers, 'Well, I'm Yiddish Dior.'

So much for the gutter. Now it's time to move over to the fast lane and see what is happening up in fashionable Blackheath, where John Schlesinger, continuing his examination of social mores, has zoomed in on a group of affluent trendies. *Sunday, Bloody Sunday* is John's *Women in Love*, or to be more exact, *A Man and a Woman in love with the Same Man*. His film had some things in common with mine – the same lighting cameraman, the same production designer and the same star, Glenda Jackson. Even her hair was a similar cut. There was only one major difference. It was false – the hair, I mean, owing to the fact that Glenda had shaved her head to play a mad woman for me in *The Music Lovers* just before John's film went into production. *Sunday, Bloody Sunday* also had some nude wrestling in front of the fire, though in retrospect I think it may have been a love scene.

But, if the homosexual overtones in *Women in Love* were only hinted at, in *Sunday, Bloody Sunday* they were put under the spotlight with Glenda's lover, Murray Head, giving gay Peter Finch a full frontal screen kiss – the first in the history of the British cinema, I believe.

Strange to say, I found the male love scenes more believable than the heterosexual episodes, one of which took place out of sight beneath the sheets and left a great deal to the imagination. There was also a feeling of *déjà vu* in some of the other scenes, where John's 'Monitor' documentary style came into play. And anyone interested in the London Telephone Exchange and Bar Mitzvahs would soon discover why everyone is always getting cut off.

Basically, the film is about time sharing, with Murray Head as the desirable property two claimants wish to occupy at the same time. In the event both parties are left out in the cold when their haven of joy moves on to greener pastures. This is all decorated with a good deal of window-dressing, in order to drape the middle-class leading characters with a cloak of reality. Trendy toddlers smoke pot and there are Sunday excursions to Greenwich Observatory to jog, fly kites, push the pram and give the dog a run – under a car. In Piccadilly we see drug users, people in fancy dress on roller skates and kids scratching the sides of cars with broken glass. There's also a lot of *Così Fan Tutte* and soft-focus photography of the male body, although I don't think this was intended to be John's answer to *Emanuelle*.

A film that set its sights even further up the social scale was *Scandal* which took the lid off the Profumo affair, a sleazy story if ever there was one. It had everything, including two notorious tarts who numbered among their clients one of Her Majesty's ministers and a member of the KGB. The girls were considered a security risk, as was the minister. After initially protesting his innocence, Profumo finally confessed to hanky-panky with the harlots and resigned. To distract attention from his misdemeanours, a scapegoat was found in the form of Stephen Ward, who organised orgies the way others organise Avon parties.

Scandal could have been a hard-hitting exposé, but what we have instead is a soft-centred fairy tale, with Ward more or less whitewashed and the police cast as the heavies, as is often the case in British films today.

A far more compelling portrait of power and corruption is to be found in *The Servant* by Joseph Losey. Black-and-white photography helps focus the attention on the personalities involved and make them stand out in sharp contrast to the background. The characters become deeply etched in the memory, thanks to Losey and his team, including the art direction of Richard MacDonald and the photography of Douglas Slocombe. The cast is faultless, with James Fox as the master and Dirk Bogarde as the manservant giving the performances of their lives. Wendy Craig as the long-suffering girlfriend and Sarah Miles as the scheming maidservant are also at the top of their form. For ensemble acting I doubt if this brilliant quartet has ever been bettered.

Likewise Harold Pinter who, when he is not trying to upstage best-selling authors, writes an immaculate screenplay. No synopsis can do justice to the insidious manner in which the master and the servant gradually become equals and exchange roles, sink into squalor and finally drown in decadence. It's about revolution, both social and cultural. It's also the best film Losey ever made, although *King and Country* runs it pretty close.

Once again this film is shot in stark black and white, and once again Losey relies on the same art director and the same star, Dirk Bogarde, to help him make a passionate statement about man's inhumanity to man.

At Hyde Park Corner, facing St George's Hospital, stands a memorial to the men of the Royal Artillery who gave their lives for King and Country in the Great War. Grim-faced monolithic Tommies cast in bronze stand guard over an unknown soldier, his face hidden beneath a helmet and his body shrouded in a cape. Towering above them, like a whited sepulchre, an enormous stone howitzer points threateningly at the sky. It is this frightening tableau that Losey uses as a background to the opening credits. A shell burst transports us to a trench on the Somme, deep in mud and human sewage. Over the top can be glimpsed barbed wire, shattered trees and the bloodied soil of no-man's-land. Below, in the dugouts, men shelter with the rats from the shrapnel that falls almost as incessantly as the rain. In an improvised cell, with part of a brass bedstead for a door, a deserter awaits trial. He tells his story to a young officer (Bogarde) who has been selected, rather against his will, to defend him.

Before he volunteered to join up, the prisoner was a cobbler who barely earned enough money to provide for his little boy and the wife who deceived him with a neighbour. Drafted to the front line, where he sees most of his mates blown to bits, there comes a moment when he can stand the shelling and the carnage no more. He explains his troubles to a sympathetic officer, who gives him an extra ration of rum, and to an unsympathetic MO, who accuses him of having cold feet and gives him a stiff dose of Number 9 – a cure for diarrhoea – and sends him back on duty. But there comes a day when the soldier just starts walking away from the guns. When he can no longer hear the firing, he gives himself up. The defending officer, who thinks the man a fool, does his best to save him, even if it makes him unpopular with his fellow officers. They know the battalion is moving up to the front the following day, and feel that it is critical to maintain morale by making an example. Accordingly the poor shell-shocked private is found guilty.

Officer: You will suffer death by shooting on Thursday the 15th of November, 1917 at 0500 hours.

Condemned Man: But sir, that's tomorrow. Anyway, you can't shoot me. I'm the last surviving member of B Company.

Everyone, officers and men alike, conspires to give him a good sendoff. The night before the execution, the boys fill him with booze and get him to play blind man's buff. He catches the padre, who absolves him of all his sins and gives him the blessed sacrament which he throws up. Comes the dawn and an injection from an officer with a hypodermic. What with the drink and the drugs, the condemned man finds it impossible to remain on his feet. Accordingly he is blindfolded again and bound to a chair, whereupon the firing squad, comprising all his friends, is given the order to *fire*. To a man they shoot to miss but they do him no favours because a few stray bullets bring him down – still bound to his chair and still very much alive. 'Isn't it finished yet?' says the defending officer, bending over him. 'No, sir, I'm sorry,' whispers the wounded man, whereupon the officer draws his revolver and administers the *coup de grâce*.

Tom Courtenay plays the condemned man with affecting simplicity and a constant belief that his superiors will exonerate him from the unjust charge of cowardice in the face of the enemy. After all, they are both on the same side, aren't they? The same side, yes, but a different class. There are those who give orders and those who obey, no matter what the circumstances. It's the old master/ servant relationship again.

It seems the class war will always be with us. If at times opposing sides unite to take arms against a common foe, it is an uneasy truce, as exemplified in the Boulting Brothers' best film *I'm All Right Jack*. Here we have bosses and workers uniting against a strike breaker, played disarmingly by Ian Carmichael. Portrayed as a hopeless case when it comes to holding down a job, Carmichael is employed by his unscrupulous family as a time and motion man in one of their factories. He soon finds that by working quicker, but not harder, he can do the work in half the time. By a simple process of deduction, his fellow workers come to the conclusion that half of them will be laid off. Inevitably, a strike follows, which is exactly what the family wants for its nefarious takeover plans.

But, in the mistaken belief that he is being loyal to his kith and kin, Carmichael carries on working, causing outrage to family and workforce alike. Despite the fact that he is sent to Coventry and subjected to all sorts of pressures, he hangs in there, and eventually becomes a national hero, appearing on TV in a live debate where he exposes both capital and labour as bigoted money-grubbers, all wanting something for nothing. By way of example, he empties out a sackful of banknotes which is blown by the air-conditioning system all over the studio floor. Debaters and audience, workers and bosses, indulge in a desperate free-for-all to get their hands on the money. This results in everyone going to court, where they are exonerated by the magistrate, with the single exception of Carmichael, who is found guilty but gets off lightly because of mental ill health brought on by overwork.

As the innocent dupe, Carmichael elevates the role of scab to the status of a folk hero while Peter Sellers as Mr Kite is the embodiment of every clap-trap trade union chief. Although his manner, as bristling as his crew cut, makes him a heavyweight on the factory floor, he's a flyweight at home. As he leaves the house on urgent union matters, his wife remarks: 'The only time you do any work is when you're on strike!' And his daughter reveals her contempt by carrying on with the scab under his own roof. With a lesser actor, Mr Kite would have been a crass caricature, but Sellers makes him credible – funny, outrageous, pathetic and sympathetic by turns.

Another great comedy actor gave an equally impressive performance in a film with a similar theme. In *The Man in the White Suit* Alec Guinness played a cranky scientist who invents a man-made fibre that is stain-proof and never wears out. At first everyone is delighted. No more dry cleaning bills and clothes that last for ever. Shock, panic, horror. The entire world economy is based on built-in obsolescence. When both capital and labour realise their livelihood is threatened they gang up on Guinness in a big way. Even his old charwoman has a go at him: 'Why can't you scientists leave things alone? What about my bit of washing when there's no washing to do?' The big industrialist who employs Guinness even gets his daughter to try to seduce him into destroying the secret formula. But, being a true Brit, he remains true to his penis and his principles and refuses to succumb. However, one winter night he gets his comeuppance in a lonely cul-de-sac, where there is no escape and nowhere to hide. A man in a white suit is a vulnerable target at the best of times. Inexorably, the mob closes in on him and, as someone grabs the lapel of the offending suit, it comes away in his hand. Disbelief and amazement quickly give way to ridicule as the white suit begins to fall apart before our very eyes – leaving Guinness standing defenceless in shirt and underwear – no longer a threat to anyone. The mocking laughter subsides, giving way to pity as Guinness makes his way through the silent crowd. One compassionate soul hands him a raincoat – an old raincoat which will eventually end up on the rubbish heap. Nothing lasts for ever, except human frailty. There is a flaw in everything, even in the miracle fibre. But man must strive towards perfection, even if it is unattainable, and it is not long before Guinness is back in the laboratory, attempting the impossible.

Directed with a deft touch by Alexander Mackendrick, this deadly satire by Roger Macdougall had one of the most inventive film scores ever by Ben Frankel. Taking the original sounds of liquids bubbling away in beakers and cunningly mixing them with bassoons and a rhythm section, Frankel concocted an unforgettably witty jazz samba that in its day became a hit single.

Frankel, sadly, is a forgotten man. But, when all the great soundtrack scores rotting in the archives are dug up, re-evaluated and hopefully rerecorded for posterity, Frankel will be up there in the Top Ten, along with Arthur Bliss, William Alwyn, John Addison, William Walton, Ralph Vaughan Williams, Alan Rawsthorne, John Ireland, Arnold Bax and Brian Easdale.

XII

Peeping Powell

For the rest of my time at the BBC, I continued my biopix on composers and artists of the late-nineteenth- and early-twentieth century. They were all mould-breaking biographical studies, told in a cinematic style which mirrored the nature of the subject under review. *Bartok* was nocturnal, mysterious, violent and expressionistic; *Isadora Duncan* was exuberant, choreographic, humanistic and celebratory; *Debussy* was dreamy, impressionistic and ambiguous; *Henri Rousseau* was primitive; *Delius* was obsessive, claustrophobic, hedonistic and monochromatic.

All the biopix, which were really feature films masquerading under the banner of TV documentaries, were shot in black and white, which gave them an added and, at times, almost newsreel-like immediacy and authenticity. The grand exception to the rule was the last film I made for the BBC, which was a Kodacolor extravaganza on the life of Richard Strauss. Subtitled 'The Dance of the Seven Veils', it portrayed the composer as an amalgam of the characters portrayed in his music, including Don Juan and Zarathustra the Superman, then stripped them away one by one to reveal the Nazi underneath.

Strauss had an inflated sense of his own importance, as his self-portraits in music testify. These include *A Hero's Life*, in which Strauss uses a mammoth symphony orchestra to demolish the critics, and the *Domestic Symphony*, in which he uses an even bigger orchestra to depict baby Strauss's bath night. Such an ego was ripe for popping, so, using his own words and music as weapons, I obliged. The result was an irreverent comic strip, as lurid as his music. The film was greeted with both acclaim and outrage. The Strauss family were up in arms and questions were asked in the House of Commons. Huw Wheldon was even summoned to attend a Select Committee to explain how such a travesty was allowed to be aired on TV. He defended the film and my right to make it brilliantly, but I was not employed by the BBC again as a film maker for the next twenty-one years.

Part of the hullabaloo arose from the fact that I had treated a serious subject in a style that was out-and-out kitsch. But I was guilty only of reflecting on film the elements I found in the music. I wonder if that is why Michael Powell's *Tales of Hoffmann* looks the way it does?

Offenbach's score might be frothy, but it could hardly be labelled either kitsch or high camp – and that's how Powell's version of the famous operetta comes across. It says much for the likes of Spielberg and Scorsese that they found the film to be such a formative influence on their work.

The plot concerns a student called Hoffmann and three of his love affairs. From the very start, when Hoffmann serenades a group of students in a *Bierkeller*, we know that schmaltz will be on tap. As tankards are raised and thighs are slapped, we are in the 'Disneyworld' of old Bavaria. Familiar faces flit by in stagey make-up – Ludmilla Tcherina, Robert Helpmann, Moira Shearer, last seen together on the screen in *The Red Shoes*, where they were creatures of flesh and blood. Here they are grotesque theatrical caricatures posturing to Frederick Ashton's camper-than-camp choreography, while Hein Heckroth's decor is the *Schlagobers* on top of the *Sachertorte*.

The first tale is easily the best, both for the story and for the light it throws on the director. Two shady characters, Spalanzani and Dr Coppelius, make a doll called Olympia and sell Hoffmann a pair of spectacles which make her appear human. He dances with her and falls madly in love, only to discover the awful truth when the inventors quarrel over money and pull the doll to pieces.

I experienced a sinking feeling of *déjà vu* the moment I saw the twitching limbs scattered over the floor immediately after the incensed inventors had quite literally torn her apart. Where had I seen that exquisite foot twitching in a ballet shoe before? In *The Red Shoes* of course – after a Côte d'Azur express had cut off Moira Shearer's feet following a grand jeté on to the railway track at Monte Carlo. As I recalled that poignant scene, a line from an old pop song came back to me: 'You always hurt the one you love, the one you shouldn't hurt at all.' Could this have been a case of unrequited love? Could this cold-blooded mutilation of the classic beauty of the red-headed ballerina be an expression of a director's thwarted passion?

Shearer's grisly death in both movies might have been pure coincidence, until one recalls what happens to her in *Peeping Tom* – Powell's masterpiece. Here she is brutally murdered by a 'would-be director' in a deserted film studio. The lethal instrument which brings about her demise is a dagger concealed in a tripod leg, which pierces her throat as the camera to which it is attached films her agonised death throes, also witnessed by the victim herself in a distorting mirror fitted around the lens.

Did Powell have it in for Moira, or was this succession of brutal deaths nothing more than a sick joke? I suppose we could ask the victim herself, though I doubt she'd tell – if indeed there was anything to tell. But a mystery persists, nevertheless. Why did Powell make the film in the first place? In doing so, he engineered his own suicide. As far as his directing career in England was concerned, he was dead. Has any other director in the history of the cinema been buried by one of his own movies? Quite a number of directors, myself included, have damaged our reputations with flops from time to time, but I doubt that our injuries (not always self-inflicted) have proved terminal.

The fact that Powell's film is all about film-making intensifies the suspicion that the suicide was premeditated. And the fact that his partner, Emeric Pressburger, wanted no part of the affair deepens the enigma.

We've already noted Powell's sympathy with the nutter in *A Canterbury Tale* who pours glue over the unprotected heads of innocent women and we've touched on the fate of the nun in the jumbo flying boots, whose sexual appetite leads her to take a nose dive down a deep ravine in Tibet. Nor should we forget the disused mineshaft in Wales down which the wanton Hazel plunges to her death in *Gone to Earth*. Now, closer to home, we have sexual retribution in Soho, where *Peeping Tom* opens. It's obviously supposed to be Soho, but actually it's a studio set making only a half-hearted attempt to look real. It's almost as if Powell is deliberately setting out to play games with us.

A prostitute stares straight into the lens and says, 'That'll be two quid.' The camera – hand held – follows her through a doorway and upstairs to a squalid room where she gets on the bed, and the tripod leg, enclosing a lethal flick-knife, comes up into frame and does the business as we track into the girl's distorted, screaming mouth. Next we see the homicidal *auteur*, played by Carl Boehm, screening the rushes in the attic of the rambling old family home he has converted into flats. Whether Powell had a private projection room in his house I cannot say, but it is not outside the bounds of possibility. A number of directors do.

Our cracked cineaste's next victim is Milly, a 'model' with a harelip whom he encounters in a studio above a porno shop. Milly's lip is as phoney as the rooftops, seen through the studio window. And her acting is as over the top as that of Miles Malleson, who makes a cameo appearance as a customer drooling over the under-the-counter girlie mags which are really no naughtier than the pix I used to supply to *Men Only* in my days as a photographer of nude women. Back in his attic flat, Carl shows home movies to one of his lodgers, a plain-looking girl in search of a boyfriend. But what she observes on the flickering screen is hardly conducive to romance.

In harsh black and white she sees a little boy sitting on a wall watching a couple make love in the park. Then she sees the same little boy asleep in his bed at night – his face illuminated by the beam of a torch. A lizard is thrown on to his chest. The boy wakes up screaming. The boy's mother is then seen lying dead on the bed. Enter a glamorous new woman into his widowed father's life, who takes home movies of the momentous day when Dad gives the luckless boy a movie camera of his own. All this disturbs the lady lodger more than somewhat, and, switching off the projector, she gets out of the darkroom, fast.

In the adjacent sitting room over coffee, Carl, who has a thick German accent and blond hair (in contrast to the dark-haired boy in the movie), explains to the frightened girl that his father wanted a cinematic record of a growing child, and that he was interested in the reaction of the nervous system to fear – especially fear in children. 'I'd wake up screaming and he'd be there taking notes and pictures,' he tells the open-mouthed girl.

When one realises that the luckless child subjected to the sadistic experiment was his own son, and that Powell played the father, the mind begins to boggle.

We now cut to Pinewood Studios, where Powell made most of his films, and where his psychotic hero works as a focus puller. Like most focus pullers, he is ambitious. He wants to be a director. Or at least that's what the gullible Miss Shearer is led to believe. This time Powell has cast her as a 'stand-in' working on the same film as our psychotic hero, who has talked her into appearing in a film of his own. One day after work they both stay behind to shoot a little surreptitious footage, knowing that if they get found out they will be fired.

'Oh, well,' says Moira, 'they can only hang you once.'

'Exactly,' replies Carl heavily.

And while he sets the lamps, Moira listens to some terrible bebop on her portable tape deck and bops around the studio in a natty pair of slacks doing a terribly 'with it' routine. 'With it' for 1960 perhaps. Funny how the *Red Shoes* ballet, made several years earlier, has not dated at all, but I guess that's the difference between pop and classical. And while Moira does her best to impersonate a cool cat, Carl is already clutching his lethal weapon and smiling in anticipation of the final take.

'I'm ready now, Viv. Will you stand over there, please.'

'Yes sir, Mr Director, sir,' replies Viv with a smile, as she hurries to her mark. About now, Brian Easdale's old jungle drums start throbbing, much as they throbbed in *Black Narcissus* and *Gone to Earth*. The director seems to be signalling that something primitive is about to happen. It does – when Viv gets it in the throat with the sharp end of the tripod, and tumbles screaming into a convenient cabin trunk. Cut to the same spot the next day where Carl is measuring up distances with a smile on his face. Everyone is getting ready for a take. The director is engaged in a meaningful discussion with one of the actors.

'The thing about this scene is that I want some comedy in it,' he says.

'But I don't feel it,' protests the actor.

'Then just do it,' shouts the director. 'Action!'

The actor, playing the manager of a luggage emporium, opens the cabin trunk for a customer who, at the sight of the stiff, promptly passes out.

'Silly bitch,' mumbles the director. 'She's fainted in the wrong place.'

Whether filming was suspended for the day I don't recall. Probably not. Filming never stops for any reason unless it's a sure-fire insurance claim.

On returning to his attic that night, Carl finds the lady lodger screening his snuff movies.

'Horrible,' she says, 'but it's just a film, isn't it?'

'No,' he says, 'I killed them.' The girl stares at him in shock. 'Do you know what the most frightening thing in the world is? This fear? When they felt the spike touching their throats and knowing it was going to kill them. They saw their own terror reflected in the mirror as the spike went in. And if death has a face they saw that too.'

He then switches on a whole bank of tape machines playing back recordings of himself as a child, screaming – aged five, screaming aged six, seven, eight, nine, ten, all screaming, screaming, screaming together – pathetic, disturbing, terrifying. Then follows the psychotic focus puller's suicide, exiting the same way as his victims, with a dagger in his throat as the cine camera records the event for posterity and the girl freaks out and the father's voice on the tape recorder says, 'Don't be a silly boy.' The child's reply, 'Goodnight, Daddy, please hold my hand,' is the most chilling final line in any film I know.

Michael Powell seems to have had a pitch-black sense of humour, and probably laughed all the way to the dole queue for, as I mentioned before, he never worked again in England on a feature film. Who knows what other delights he had in store for Moira Shearer?

There was a time when Powell's attitude to the women in his films was less bent. Wendy Hiller in *I Know Where I'm Going* was a no-nonsense young person who knew she wanted to marry the millionaire who had invited her to join him on a private island off the west coast of Scotland. The opening of the film is a cinematic tour de force with Wendy, in glamorous garb, saying goodbye to Daddy at a *thé dansant* in some never-never art deco metropolitan hotel. The score imitates Fred and Ginger's Hollywood, with swooning saxes and a heavenly choir crooning 'I know where I'm going', on the soundtrack.

After a witty dream sequence, in which our heroine imagines her future life of luxury, there follows a highly organised journey to Scotland, courtesy of her intended. This includes one moment of utter joy when a station master's top hat imperceptibly turns into the puffing funnel of the express train speeding Wendy to the Highlands. But a blanket of Scottish mist causes the meeting to be postponed, leaving Wendy stranded on the mainland and forced to put up in the local hotel. Here she meets and falls for a local lad, played by Roger Livesey. At first she resists her true feelings, imagining him to be honest but poor. But, by the time the fog disperses, she has learnt that her elusive 'millionaire' is only renting the house on the island from Roger Livesey, who turns out to be the laird in lad's clothing. When she finally does cross the water, she does so arm in arm with her young Scottish lover.

So ends the most magical romantic comedy ever made in England. If we hadn't read the credits, we could be forgiven for imagining the hand of a great American director, such as Preston Sturges or Billy Wilder, to be at work here, so sure is the style, so witty the telling of the tale. See this film and weep. You will never see its like again.

But to continue the theme of the eternal female in the films of Michael Powell. It seems that he not only liked them dead but also dolled up in uniform. Kim Hunter looked very dishy indeed in her outfit in *A Matter of Life and Death*, one of Powell's most imaginative, if silly, films. I cannot recall whether she was a WAAF or a GI in the US airforce, but, as she was an American actress appearing in a British movie, it was probably the latter. Either way, she falls for the voice of a wounded English pilot plunging to his doom in a flaming Lancaster over the Kent coast during the last war. The pilot, played with tremendous dash by David Niven, begins to fall for her too, as she tries to get a fix on his position and tells him her name is June. But it can't last.

'I'm bailing out – without a parachute,' shouts Niven above the roar of the flames and the screaming of the engines. 'And June . . . if you're around when they pick me up, turn your head away.'

Come the dawn, we find Niven stumbling ashore, looking as if he's just swum the channel in a fur-lined flying suit. He staggers over the dunes where he encounters a naked boy sitting on the sand, with his legs firmly crossed, playing a flute to a rather puzzled goat. After which, Niven faints. Leaving us to wonder how a wounded man can fall a thousand feet into the sea and survive. Is it a miracle? No, it is a mistake. The computers in heaven have cocked up, allowing a man who should be dead to remain precariously alive. But justice must be done. As Niven hovers between life and death on the operating table, he is put on trial, in absentia, in that great Courthouse in the sky which, according to the director, is a gigantic, monochromatic amphitheatre full of dead soldiers of both sexes. To my eye, it looked very dull indeed, an opinion evidently shared by Marius Goring as Robespierre when he comes down to earth to advise the accused. 'One is starved for Technicolor up there,' he observes, metamorphosing from black and white to colour in front of a rhododendron bush, the shade of his bright ruby lips.

Apart from Marius Goring's make-up, complete with beauty spot, the most spectacular thing in the entire film is the giant escalator connecting the pilot's subconscious mind, as he lies on the operating table, to the celestial Courthouse. Fifty feet wide and God alone knows how high, it provides the weirdest form of space travel ever shown in a movie – zapping its shadowy passengers through time and space at the incredible rate of one and a half miles an hour. (Three decades later London Transport's underground has gone one better – in perfecting escalators that do not move at all.)

So what is the verdict of this heavenly court of appeal? The pranged pilot gets off, of course. He gets off the operating table and gets off with the girl.

Kathleen Byron plays the uniformed receptionist at the Purgatory Hilton, handing out angel wings in exchange for propellers carried by the deceased airmen who check in. We last saw her as the demented nun taking a nose dive down a ravine, while the Reverend Mother rang the Angelus, in *Black Narcissus*. Unfortunately, we are not permitted a peep behind the counter to see if she is still wearing those king-size flying boots.

Was this Powell having a little harmless fun again? If so, it seems that no one noticed. And I doubt if many spotted a glaring continuity error in *The Life and Death of Colonel Blimp*. It comes near the beginning of the film, when the hero and heroine are getting acquainted in a Berlin café. Between them, in the centre of the table, stands a large candelabra. At least it is there in the long shot, but vanishes, as if by magic, whenever we cut closer. In a short scene, Powell might have got away with it. But this sequence of interminable dialogue lasts an entire reel. Perhaps he knew this was the most deadly conversation he'd ever filmed and sought to liven it up a bit with the disappearing and reappearing candelabra. But, if this was not the case, the continuity girl should have been fired.

The girl at the café table, by the way, was none other than the Mother Superior herself, Deborah Kerr, playing another part or, to be more precise, three other parts. Obviously, Powell couldn't get enough of her, but that's another story . . .

Powell died in 1992 – praised by many of those who had buried him. The last time I saw him he was an exile in Hollywood working as a 'tea boy' for Francis Ford Coppola.

XIII

Basket Case

Thinking of continuity howlers, there was a beaut in *Fire over England*, where Queen Elizabeth's venerable Lord Chancellor totters out of one room in a long, spatular beard and enters the next in a short, forked one. Today, one would certainly consider a reshoot, but William K. Howard, the director, let it go. Maybe they were not always so fussy about such things in the days of black & white. Apart from the Lord Chancellor's beard, the film is of considerable historical interest, because it was made around the time of the Spanish Civil War, and is both prophetic and propagandist. A subtitle puts us in the picture. '1857 – Spain powerful in the Old World, Master of the New. Its King – Philip, rules the world by force and fear. Spanish tyranny is challenged by the free people of a little island – England.'

One of these free people is Laurence Olivier, playing a loyal subject of good Queen Bess, despatched to enemy territory as a spy. He must pass himself off as a traitor, in the hope of soliciting from bad King Philip the identity of the real traitors plotting the downfall of their virgin queen. Predictably, Olivier's ship is attacked en route, giving our hero an opportunity to swing on ropes as models burn and extras jump from yardarms into the studio tank. Olivier dives in after them and strikes out. A quick dissolve and his double is staggering ashore in Sunny Spain – though it looks more like Bognor Regis and probably was. Moments later in Madrid, Olivier bumps into a Spanish beauty, who happens to be an old flame. Will she betray him? Will she, billyo! But he's rumbled regardless, and has to beat it, though not before he has tricked the names of the traitors from the lips of the King himself, who is not amused at the deception. Neither is the old flame's husband. 'Treating enemies like human beings . . .' he says to his errant wife with a scowl. 'Don't you see what that leads to? It leads to the end of Patriotism, the end of war, the end of everything!' Yea, verily, and, before you know it, Olivier has returned to England, unmasked the traitors, defeated the Armada and married the girl – Vivien Leigh, no less. Flora Robson and Raymond Massey also starred as the respective tyrants – all royally served by the majestic photography of James Wong Howe.

Well, we won that one, due largely to our own appalling weather. And, in clipping Spain's territorial wings, Great Britain began to spread her own.

Good Queen Bess has featured in several epics, including Hollywood's: *Elizabeth and Essex* with Bette Davis and Errol Flynn playing the leads. But the definitive version remains to be made, possibly by my old mate Derek Jarman, proving that the old Queen was either a lesbian or a transvestite or possibly both. Tilda Swinton won't know which way to turn.

What other British monarchs have commanded audiences at the box office, I wonder? Henry VIII probably tops the list, with Charles Laughton way out in front of any other impersonators, and Keith Michell sagging behind with a surfeit of padding, in his cheeks and round his belly. Then, of course, there are the Royals associated with Shakespeare, immortalised by the great Olivier, whose sovereignty was called into question when he was completely outclassed by Marilyn Monroe in *The Prince and the Showgirl*.

At the back of my mind, I have a picture of King Harold with an arrow in his eye, but that might well have been a reconstruction served up for TV by the late, lamented Benny Hill. What of King Canute and King Alfred? I'm sure they are worthy subjects, but a couple of two-hour epics culminating in a pair of wet feet and a tray of blackened fairy cakes is hardly the stuff of Boffo Box Office.

King Arthur is another matter. Instead of cakes we have tarts, and very tasty ones, at that. Guinevere, Arthur's dishy wife, betrays him with his best friend, Lancelot, and in turn the King betrays her with his half sister Morgan Le Fay – at least, that is what happened according to John Boorman's *Excalibur*. This evocation of the legends surrounding King Arthur is far more convincing than Hollywood's assembly-line version of *The Knights of the Round Table*, featuring Robert Taylor. Boorman's film is hand crafted and, for the most part, bears the stamp of an individual artist. The story has the quality of a medieval tapestry as reflected in the shimmering mirror of the Lady of Shalott. This is largely thanks to the dazzling photography of Alex Thomson and the brilliant costumes of Bob Ringwood. Never has armour glittered so brightly or symbolised so boldly the high ideals of the Arthurian brotherhood. By comparison, the performances are closer to pewter than polished steel. The exception is Boorman's son (who grew into the teenage Tommy in *The Emerald Forest*), attired here in armour of burnished gold. He speaks with natural grace, whereas the rest of the lookalike knights talk like the giant in *Jack and the Beanstalk*.

Apart from a startling overhead shot of a knight in armour rutting with a naked woman, the film owes a lot to Disney, and is none the worse for that. There are times when it would not be a surprise to see Bambi come bouncing into the mossy glades. (And didn't Disney also make *The Sword in the Stone*?) And where have I seen that Hall of the Holy Grail before? Not in Disneyland, but the Land of Oz, another old favourite of John's if I'm not mistaken. Yes, it's the Emerald City again. But there is also some remarkable imagery that is pure Boorman – think of the knights who have failed in their quest for the Holy Grail, hanging lifeless in their rusting armour from the branches of an enormous, decaying tree. Then there's a disgraced and wounded knight, shaking off his armour to save himself from drowning, and inadvertently receiving the sacrament of baptism at the same time.

Armour, as anyone knows who has attempted to lift King Henry VIII's stainless steel codpiece, is very heavy. Too heavy for the lithe steeds that speed our knights in shining plastic through their many adventures. Carthorses would have been more in order only they are less glamorous and fleet of foot and, after all, John was not making a documentary, but dreaming a dream of chivalry.

As the sun sinks slowly in the west, the vessel bearing the body of the dead king sails across the darkening seas to Avalon – the mystic isle somewhere over the horizon that I believe John himself is searching for.

The first royal family to be enshrined in a decent picture was Queen Victoria's – although, paradoxically, in *Victoria the Great* it was kept something of a secret.

In this film it would appear that Victoria had only one daughter –Alice, instead of the baker's dozen familiar to us all from those old sepia photographs of the period. Maybe it's just as well that Albert died when he did, or there would be even more of their progeny around today, sponging off the public. At least the lives of Mum and Dad seemed blessedly free from scandal. Indeed, they were a worthy couple, according to the director, Herbert Wilcox, who was of course married to the Queen at the time. The Queen I'm referring to is that one-time queen of the British screen, HM Anna Neagle. Here she plays the great lady as if on ball bearings with a stick up her crinoline, gliding stiffly around the corridors of Buckingham Palace.

However, in her more private moments, she is far more relaxed. When she is bathing the dog in her bedroom on the morning of her coronation, she remains oblivious to the cries of the impatient crowds below. I wonder if our own dear Queen did the same with the royal Corgis.

Certain things never change – the ceremony in the Abbey, the twenty-one gun salute, the pealing of the bells and the cheering of the mob. We get this traditional montage throughout the film whenever there is an event full of Pomp and Circumstance – like a Royal Wedding.

The Queen's consort is played here by Anton Walbrook, with an air of easy detachment which masks feelings of deep concern. The finesse and quiet wit he brought to the majority of his roles is also much in evidence here. What a great actor he was and greatly underrated too. Anna was no slouch either.

The proposal scene in the palace is beautifully judged by both of them.

'He would never take the liberty to propose,' the young Victoria murmurs to herself as she awaits the arrival of the handsome young suitor Albert of Saxe, Coburg and Gotha. 'I must propose myself.'

Albert is announced, enters and bows nervously, knowing full well why he has been summoned to the Royal presence.

'Albert, you have gained my whole heart,' says Victoria, simply. 'It would make me very happy if you would consent to spend your life with me.'

The Prince is understandably stunned. The Queen misreads this as reticence and becomes a little hesitant herself. 'If you could make that sacrifice . . .?'

Albert, who has fallen under her spell, is appalled. 'Sacrifice? But I feel so unworthy.'

Victoria is equally moved. 'How can you say that?' She indicates that he should join her on the sofa. 'It quite bewilders me that you should love me.'

He is emboldened to take her hand. 'I will do everything in my power to make you happy.'

They embrace. Churchbells! You believe it.

You also believe their relationship after the honeymoon, during which they sing Schubert. As consort, Albert wants to help her in affairs of state. But she looks upon him as a toy boy rather than an intellectual equal. So, she runs the country while he runs her parties, until after an outrageous display of bad manners on her part he throws down the gauntlet by breaking the No Smoking ban in the Palace and lights up a formidable meerschaum pipe. 'Send for his Highness,' commands the Queen, having got a knockout whiff of the fumes from the music room, where the Prince has just been enveloping Mendelssohn in clouds of tobacco smoke. The Prince declines the invitation to have his ear chewed off. Astounded by this breach of protocol, the Queen stomps off in search of her husband, only to find him in the bedroom behind a locked door.

'Albert, I sent for you; why didn't you come?' she cries.
SILENCE
Victoria knocks on the door. 'Open up, it's the Queen.'
SILENCE
Victoria rattles the handle: 'Open up, it's Victoria.'
SILENCE
Victoria, cooing: 'Albert, it's your wife.'
SILENCE
Then there is a click as the door opens and Victoria demurely braves the pipe smoke, softly closing the door behind her. From that moment – according to the script – Victoria allowed Albert to share the burden of government. We see them help repeal the Corn Laws and prevent a headstrong Prime Minister from declaring war on America. That's about it, before Albert kicks the bucket and the widow of Windsor goes into permanent mourning.

She spends the rest of the film looking pretty glum. And so, no doubt, would you if you only had a Scottish gillie for company and were given a terrible white wig to wear.

The reign comes to an end with the Queen's Diamond Jubilee, when, to the usual montage of bells, cheers, and gunfire, Victoria gets in her carriage, puts up her parasol and goes to town. Somewhere along the way I seem to remember a subtitle reading '30 years later'. I think it was here that Wilcox gave up the struggle.

Victoria the Great is neither an intimate portrait nor a teeming canvas. Heck, we've got a character here the equal of Cleopatra. What am I saying, equal? Victoria's Empire was a thousand times greater, and you only have to consider the size of their respective families and the monument Victoria built to her lover's memory to complete the comparison. If you look at the south-eastern tableau of the Albert memorial, you'll actually see Cleopatra, reduced to the status of a slave girl tending a camel. That says it all. Pity Wilcox didn't have the same budget as Mankiewicz's Hollywood epic. As everybody who has seen newsreel footage of Victoria's funeral knows, it makes Cleopatra's ceremonial entry into Rome look like a tawdry carnival.

It is tempting to wonder what Elizabeth Taylor and Richard Burton would have made of Victoria and Albert. Idle speculation! As it is, Anna Neagle and Anton Walbrook make an extremely credible royal couple. If the present royal family is to survive as a marketable commodity, they will simply have to act better, or others will do it for them.

The 'Tampax kid' may survive the 'soaps' about his marital problems and even be crowned king. But what if his life is cut short? These are dangerous times, and he may not be as lucky as his great, great grandmama, who escaped an assassin's bullet by inches. Martyred, he would become instantly bankable, perfect material for a Hollywood biopic in the style of *JFK* or *Gandhi*. In which case, let us hope that Sir Richard Attenborough is still around to administer the kiss of death.

On the other hand, I suppose HRH the Prince of Wales could simply abdicate like the Duke of Windsor, and hope he gets a mini-series. As King he could end up like one of his illustrious ancestors – with his head in a basket. The country could be run again by a Lord Protector. Richard Harris played the last one, and very good he was too.

Hardly less good was Alec Guinness as the misguided King Charles I. The commoner was intense and rhetorical, the monarch withdrawn and intransigent. Both men were self-assured and self-righteous, because both had God on their side. It was their modes of worship that were irreconcilable. Charles was High Church and high-handed. If Parliament challenged his will, Parliament was dissolved. Such is the state of affairs when *Cromwell* opens, with Parliament reconvened after twelve years, in order to grant the King more money to finance war against the Scottish rebels marching on Newcastle.

Far from it being the mere formality he expects, the King is granted his request on the condition (proposed by Cromwell and the Puritans) that he relinquish all power over Parliament – which in effect should govern the country. His refusal to agree to this demand leads the country to civil war. The first battle is a rout – the King's troops and the sons of gentlemen armed with muskets on one side, and untrained yeomen equipped with pikes on the other.

'The war will not be won by farmers. I will have to raise an army of hand-picked men the like of which this land has never seen,' vows Cromwell. And by the dawning of the battle of Naseby he has achieved just that. 'Trust in God and keep your powder dry,' he roars, leading the cavalry charge. Despite the rebels being greatly outnumbered, the day ends in victory for them and signals the turning point of the war. With the fall of Bristol, all hope is gone and the King capitulates.

'You are under arrest by order of Parliament,' Cromwell informs him.

'I know no power higher than the authority of the King,' replies the monarch.

'It was on that issue the war was fought,' Cromwell reminds him.

An illegal trial follows and the King is found guilty of treason and condemned to death. The decision of the jury is by no means unanimous, but Cromwell has the last word as the King's head drops in the basket. 'The office of the King is now abolished. Long live Parliament, Long live the Republic.'

But the victors squabble among themselves until Cromwell, now Commander in Chief of the Army, marches into the House at the head of his troops. 'Instead of uniting the good people of this nation we have anarchy, corruption, division and dissatisfaction. The enemies of the nation have flourished. An immoral parliament is more obnoxious than an immoral king. You are scum. I hereby declare this Parliament dissolved.' He picks up the mace and tosses it aside. 'Away with this bauble. The nation will be justly governed.' And as his troops force everyone to leave the House, Cromwell declares: 'I will deliver men's souls. There will be a golden age of learning and the law will be for everyone. I swear by God I will see this nation properly governed, even if I have to do it myself.'

And sure enough, he was true to his word, as we are reminded by the last subtitle:

'Cromwell became Lord Protector of England for five years until his death in 1658. Three years later Charles II was crowned King.'

So ends one of the most thought-provoking films ever produced in this country, and even more relevant today than when it was made back in 1970 when the monarchy seemed set fair to be the prime exhibits in Madame Tussaud's for ever.

So much for the potted history. What about the film? Without doubt it is a major achievement, and if Maurice Jarre had composed the musical score, it might have been recognised as such. Written and directed by Ken Hughes with authority and a fine eye for period detail, the story of Cromwell is told in a well-paced succession of cliffhangers right up to the big chop and beyond. The two big battles are the equal of anything in Bondarchuk's *Waterloo*, and, if they don't quite match those in

King Vidor's *War and Peace*, that is probably because Hughes had neither the budget nor the Red Army at his disposal.

The dialogue is also well judged, and not without its moments of poignant humour – as when the King is dressing for the last time.

KING: How will I be conveyed to the place of execution – by carriage?

GUARD: No, your Majesty, you will go on foot.

KING: Excellent, the walk will do me good. Is it chilly out today?

GUARD: Yes, it's cold, your majesty.

KING: Then I am glad I put on a second shirt. I would not have the people think I was trembling through fear.

Even on the scaffold, the King conducts himself with dignity. 'I go from a corruptible crown to an incorruptible crown and everlasting peace.' Obviously not a bad man, he loved England in his way, but was completely out of touch with the people. How little some things have changed in the last three hundred years in our native land.

XIV

The Natives Are Restless

There is a tendency in films dealing with natives, of any colour, to make them look too damn clean. That was certainly the case in *The Mission*. It was also true of *Gandhi*, directed by Sir Richard Attenborough. Nearly everyone appeared freshly washed, and wore a pretty little sari with a fringe on the top. *Gandhi* looks as if it's been made for the Indian tourist board. The screen teems with bright-eyed children in Persil white. Venerable gentlemen with silver beards meditate quietly, as brutal red-faced British troops march up and down, barking orders and barking mad.

Apart from the odd massacre, the Brits, who are naturally cast as the baddies, crumble before the charm of the Mahatma – civil servants and soldiers alike. Even the antagonistic General Smuts caves in and gives him a shilling for a taxi. But Gandhi's crusade for a free India is a story worth telling, and, although Attenborough seems bent on showing the worst side of the British administration, the result is a real achievement. Organising ten extras can be tough enough but getting 50,000 to cry on cue is something of a miracle. However, the grief expressed by the extras for the re-enactment of Gandhi's funeral procession is somewhat strained. Apparently, most of them had never heard of him – and, by the time the cameras were finally ready to roll after a five-hour line-up, everyone was dying to go for a pee. When the shot was finally in the can and Dickie cried 'Cut!', it was like the Relief of Mafeking.

I vividly remember seeing an amateur movie of the funeral on television. Despite the fact that it was shot at the speed of an old

Mack Sennett comedy, on substandard stock; despite the fact that the duped print was scratched and contrasty, the magic was palpable. The shimmering image of the faithful mourners fighting for a glimpse of their saviour had a visionary quality that throbbed with life and feelings.

By comparison, Attenborough's reconstruction is a very wooden affair.

But elsewhere the director has better luck with his crowd, as when they prostrate themselves in protest before a troop of mounted policemen who charge them down. The horses show more compassion than their riders, and deftly step around the would-be martyrs. A very moving sequence in a movie that for the most part is simply too respectful.

Travelling further north, the natives revealed themselves to be even less friendly in David Lean's *Lawrence of Arabia*. However, they are painted, and I use the word advisedly, as being nicer to foreigners than to their own kind. This is illustrated early in the film when a Bedouin guide and a Lieutenant Lawrence serving in HM Forces are caught by Omar Sharif drinking at his well in the middle of the desert. The Bedouin, who belongs to a rival tribe, gets a bullet in the brain while El Awrence, as the natives call the reckless Britisher, is spared. The rest of the film is devoted to showing Lawrence's efforts to unite the Arab nation to fight against the colonial ambitions of, first, Turkey, and latterly France and Great Britain.

By smooth chat and by example – he even dresses like an Arab – Lawrence not only brings two unfriendly tribes together but leads them across the uncrossable 'Sun's Anvil' to catch the Turks in the rear at Aqaba.

As an abbreviated history of the part the Arab nation played in the Great War, the film is simple but effective. In its effort to portray the complex man at the heart of the conflict, it comes a cropper.

We first see Lawrence, not as an army officer, not in his Arab robes, not in the desert but as a bareheaded corporal in the RAF riding a motorbike down a leafy country lane in England. Two errand boys larking about on pushbikes cause him to swerve. Cut to a riderless motorbike crashing into a burnt-out gorse bush. Cut to the aftermath of a funeral at St Paul's. Cut to Donald Wolfit in a top hat saying, 'He had some minor function on my staff in Cairo . . .' Cut to Cairo and the smiling Lawrence, now an officer in the army, holding a lighted match and putting it out with his finger and thumb. An admiring private tries to imitate him and gives a yelp of pain when he is burnt. 'What's the trick?' he asks. 'It hurts!'

'The trick,' replies Lawrence, still smiling, 'is not minding that it hurts.'

This almost throwaway scene is the first clue as to the true nature of Lawrence's character. From the very start he is seen as a man at odds with himself. Even on his first mission, when almost dying of thirst, he refuses to let a drop of water pass his lips until his native guide – hardened to the ways of the desert – takes the first swig.

From then on he endures pain and suffering with a stoicism that even puts the Arabs to shame, not only from the merciless grip of nature but also from the hand of man – as when he is beaten with a flayed cane in a filthy Turkish jail. In fact he seems to enjoy being tortured. This, quite naturally, begins to worry him. Acts of violence also turn him on, as when he executes an erring friend by blowing his brains all over the desert, from which Lawrence had rescued him only a few days before, putting his own life at risk. Obviously, El Awrence, the man some Arabs are beginning to deify, is a complex being. It's a pity that Lean balks at showing us just how complex. There is a scene in Cairo where General Allenby notices blood seeping through the back of Lawrence's uniform, little knowing it is a souvenir of his night in

Left: The kiss.
*Sunday, Bloody
Sunday*

Below: Scandal

Locked out. Peter Sellers as Mr Pike, the shop steward, in *I'm All Right, Jack*

Dirk Bogarde. From *The Servant* to an officer and a gentleman in *King and Country*

A Matter of Life and Death

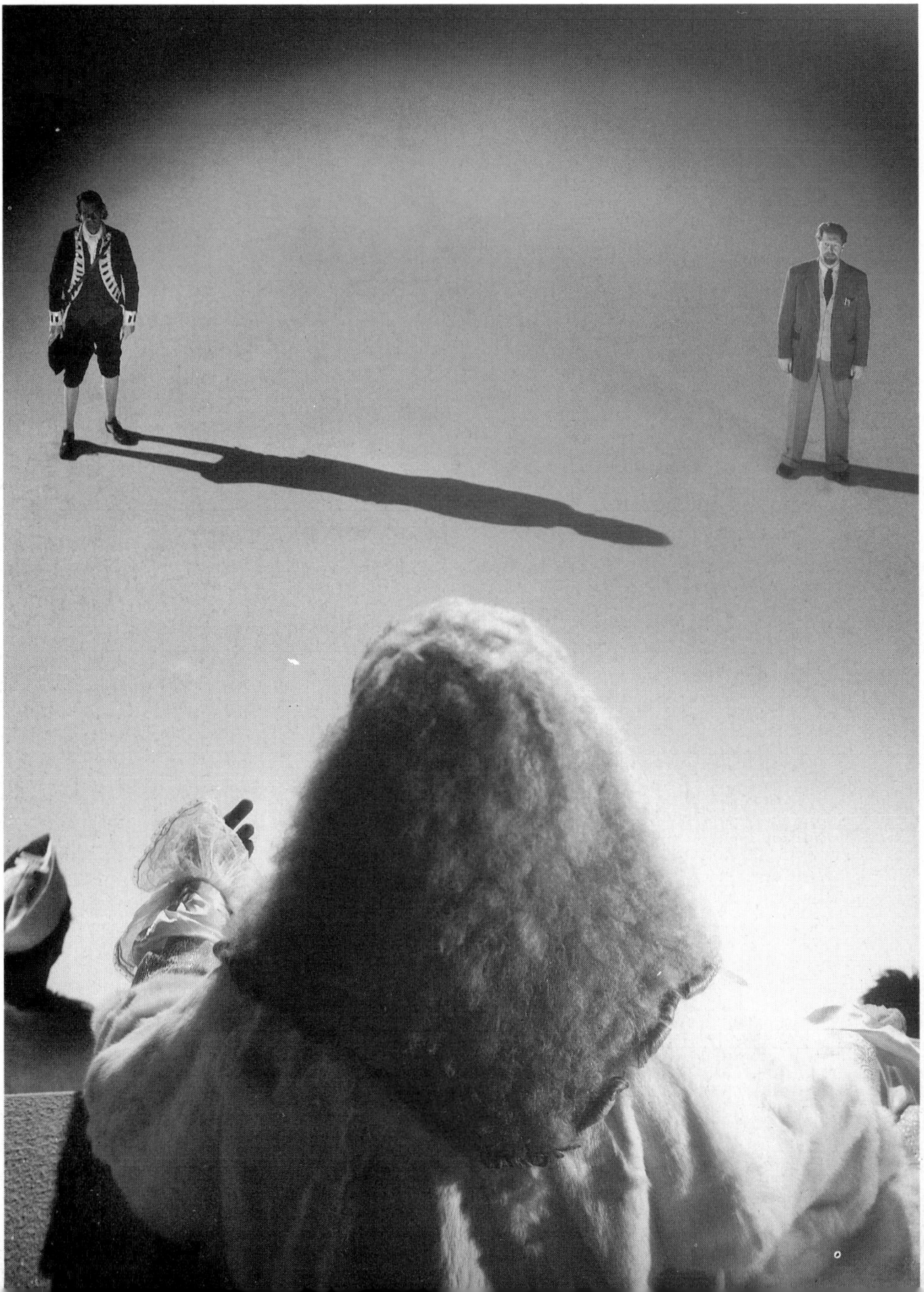

Fire Over England

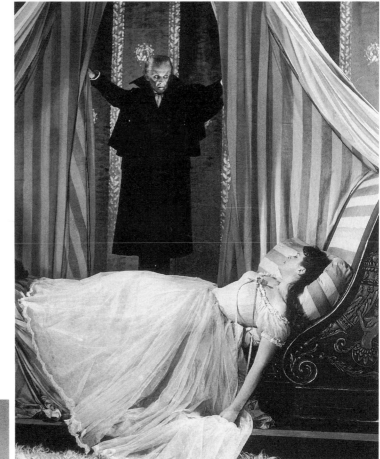

Left: Home movies,
XX certificate.
Peeping Tom

*Right: Tales of
Hoffman*

*Below left: Victoria
the Great*

Below: Excalibur

Two enemies of the Raj saddle up on Blockbuster. *Cromwell* and *Gandhi*

the Turkish jail. Shocked, Allenby asks if he is seeing a doctor. Lawrence shakes his head. 'Tell me what happened,' says Allenby. Lawrence opens his mouth to do so and we cut to an unrelated scene.

Earlier in the film, Lawrence admitted to Allenby that he had enjoyed executing his friend, so further discussion of the subject was quite in order and promised to be revealing. Was it shot and never used or simply never shot? Did Hollywood step in with the scissors or did Lean just chicken out? What we get instead is growing paranoia, and an insistence from Lawrence that he is an ordinary man who wants an ordinary life with an ordinary job.

With the capture of Damascus and the disintegration of the Arab people, who fail to capitalise on their brief victory, Lawrence returns to England, presumably a disillusioned man. 'You're lucky,' says the corporal driving Lawrence to his ship, 'you're going home.' Lawrence smiles ironically through the swirling sand thrown up by the vehicle in front of them, for the desert is Lawrence's real home and he is leaving it – to die on a motorbike wearing the uniform of a corporal in the Royal Air Force. We never learn why he was transferred from the Army. THE END bangs on the screen just as the story promises to get interesting. The sands of time have run out. Surely three and a half hours is long enough to tell Lawrence's story, unless like him you are in love with the desert.

David Lean obviously shared his passion, lingering over innumerable shots of sand dunes. And one of the most lush love themes ever written for the cinema is reserved for the voluptuous landscape that constantly reclines seductively across the wide, wide screen. People become secondary to sand, and it is to the credit of Peter O'Toole that we comprehend the complexity of Lawrence as much as we do. Whether striding along the roof of a derailed train in his elegant white robes with the arrogance of a model at a Parisian fashion show, or riding hunched, desperate and travel-stained in the same outfit on a dirty camel, his portrayal of a tormented man is outstanding.

O'Toole is supported by a splendid cast. Particularly commendable, as a couple of swarthy Arabs, are Anthony Quinn and Alec Guinness, who overcome their cocoa make-up and false noses to match the more authentic excellence of Omar Sharif. But it is a pity Lean didn't make a sequel called *Lawrence of Dorset*, where I believe our lad ended up. It would be fascinating to find out a little more about the relationship between the homosexual airman and those cheeky errand boys on bicycles Lawrence tried so hard to avoid on his motorbike.

Apart from Lawrence's unresolvable inner conflict, the film also illustrates the problems that arise when an advanced civilisation comes into violent contact with a primitive one – more advanced in the ways of destruction, that is.

John Boorman also examines a similar phenomenon in *The Emerald Forest*. Armoured cars and heavy artillery may have given way to bulldozers and excavators but the impact on the natives is much the same, as the juggernaut of civilisation rolls remorselessly through South American rainforests, obliterating the people who have lived there longer than anyone can remember.

Boorman's approach to this human tragedy is ingenious. An engineer working on the construction of an enormous dam takes his wife and toddler, Tommy, on a picnic at the edge of the jungle. Tommy toddles into the trees and in the twinkling of an eye – disappears. Twelve years later Dad is still building the dam, which is near completion, and sporadically looking for Tommy. Taking a few days off, he resumes the search in earnest, along with a brash photo journalist who is hoping for a scoop. The two-man expedition runs into trouble the moment it enters the almost impenetrable jungle. Sinister natives in frightening war paint materialise from the undergrowth. While the photographer, still snapping away, is dragged off to the cauldron, Dad makes his escape with the aid of an automatic rifle that makes mincemeat out of all the gourmet chefs who wanted to finger the meat before cooking. There follows a chase, during which Dad's life is saved (wait for it) by the sudden appearance of his son, who now wears a loincloth and fires a bow and arrow. At the moment of recognition Dad is wounded, but is saved from capture by Tommy, who drags him to safety in his native village. While Dad recuperates from his encounter with the 'Fierce People', we learn that Tommy has been brought up by the chief of the 'Invisible People', who wanted to save him from his own people, known, for obvious reasons, as the 'Termite People'.

The conflict that follows is inevitable. Dad wants to take Tommy home to Mum and the microwave, while the lad himself opts for the simple life he shares with his adopted family. And who can blame him? Frolicking with bare-breasted dusky maidens in clear mountain streams and carousing by the fire all night has to be better than slaving away in an office and watching telly. Not according to Dad. Despite the female charms on offer, he feels duty-bound to return home to his wife and his work, reluctantly leaving Tommy behind to marry his eager bride and snort jungle dust happily ever after.

But the fairy tale is over for Tommy and his tribe, when he returns from a hunting expedition one day to find that the 'Fierce People' have murdered most of the old people, including his adopted 'Daddy', and made off with all the young women, including his wife. Soon Tommy and some of his tribe (known as the 'Invisible People' because of their expertise in camouflage), track the women down to a fortified brothel set up on the edge of the jungle for the pleasure of construction workers. Repulsed by the automatic guns of the armed guards, Tommy and a friend decide to brave the dangers of the unknown city and seek out help from Dad. Tommy only has the vaguest memory of his childhood home but, after a snort of jungle dust, projects himself into the mind of an eagle circling the city. Recognising a block of flats, he sets about getting to the eleventh floor – not by landing on the roof but by re-entering his body and climbing up the face of the twenty-storey building and on to a balcony. My! Is Mum surprised to see her son in loincloth and green paint peering at her through the living-room window. But the great homecoming scene is reduced to a quick hug – and Tommy is off again, with Dad and a couple of mates, to rescue the girls from their life of sexual slavery.

A Rambo-type assault on sin city follows with the baddies killed and the righteous reconciled. The End? Not yet. We have Dad's remorse to reckon with. Realising that he is partly responsible for what has been and what will be, he decides to destroy the newly completed dam – despite the fact that Tommy has predicted that the Gods of the Forest will do the deed for him. Of course Tommy is right. The thunderclouds gather, torrential rain falls, the river floods, the dam breaks and Dad is saved from committing a crime.

The Gods of Nature have taken their revenge. And if this seems all a little fanciful, as a clever model of the dam disintegrates before our very eyes, the chances are that in reality the old Gods will have the last laugh. For even though the real dam is still very much intact and has flooded thousands of square miles of happy hunting ground, we have been made aware that the obliteration of the rainforests will bring about our self-destruction. A rolling subtitle before the final credits reminds us that for many the end has already come. It reads: 'The rainforests of the Amazons are disappearing at the rate of 5,000 acres a day. 4,000,000 Indians once lived there, 120,000 still remain. A few tribes have never had contact with the outside world. They still know what we have forgotten.'

We leave the cinema shaking our heads and tutting, just as we did when we first saw the cavalry beat the hell out of the Indians back in 1930. Times have changed. The redskins now live on reservations, smoke pot, drive Cadillacs and watch TV. Maybe some of those 3,880,000 Indians unaccounted for on Boorman's subtitle joined Tommy's father back in the big city, having grown tired of the endless round of huntin', snortin' 'n' fishin'.

Before we bid farewell to the noble savage and the land of the subtitle, try this: '1950, Kenya Colony – a movement has begun amongst the Kikuyu tribe to reclaim their land and achieve independence from the British'. In *The Kitchen Toto* the British are represented by a district commissioner and his family, and the Kikuyu by a little black boy who works for them. The 'Toto' has kitchen duties, while the decadent commissioner cheats on his wife and does his best to maintain his dwindling native police force, who are deserting in droves. Inspecting a new batch of bare-chested recruits daubed in war paint, he snaps to his sergeant, 'Get them to scrub off that ochre and get them into uniform!' The transformation from painted warriors to policemen is achieved in a single jump cut, quickly emphasising the stupidity of trying to wash away an entire culture with a bar of carbolic and a cold shower.

There follows a sad picture of yet another bloody sunset on the dwindling British Empire. Brother turns on brother and the innocent are put to the sword. No one is spared, not even the children. The commissioner's ten-year-old son has no option but to perform a mercy killing by shooting his mother in the back when she is dragged from the house by a crazed band of Kikuyu. His friend, the brave little kitchen Toto, suspected of collaborating with the enemy, is tortured by his own people.

In 1952 a state of emergency was declared in Kenya Colony. During the conflict, about 80 Europeans and 14,000 Africans were killed. 'In 1963 Kenya achieved independence,' proclaims the last subtitle. This film movingly illustrates something of the cost involved. Now, natives everywhere are free at last: free to bash each other over the head and fight religious wars just like the rest of us.

Let's have some music!

XV

That's Entertainment: Part II

About twenty years ago MGM released a feature-length film called *That's Entertainment*, with a compilation of their product spanning more than half a century. Sounds indigestible, but it was such a hit that they repeated the experiment with *That's Entertainment Part II*, which was also big at the box office. Ninety per cent of the material in these two films was related to the musical. We tend to forget that movies were invented for one purpose and one purpose only – to entertain. But nowadays the audience wants more – it wants uplift, it wants commitment, it wants a message. 'If they want a message,' said Sam Goldwyn, 'tell 'em to send for Western Union.'

But entertainment and enlightenment are not incompatible, as Alan Parker for one is always trying to prove. In *The Commitments* he succeeds. The story concerns the birth of a band in Dublin – and its short but turbulent life. The central character is a youth called Rabbitte, whose dream is to bring 'soul' to his native city. So he starts recruiting a group from his neighbourhood, which happens to be on the wrong side of the tracks – the North Side. One group member sings in a church choir and another at weddings, one works in a fish and chip van, another in a refrigeration plant as a meat packer.

Rabbitte has a hard job. The majority of the 'talent' have settled for life on the dole and all that goes with it, and those in work want to know why they should give up a steady job. 'So you can stand out from the "tossers",' shouts Rabbitte, 'and won't have to spend the rest of your life packing fucking frozen chickens.'

They have no money and no prospects, until Rabbitte starts whipping them into shape with a few sharp lessons in style and delivery. A video of Little Richard unnerves them. 'Don't you think we are a bit white for that?' asks one timid member of the group, voicing the fears of his mates. 'Bollocks,' barks Rabbitte. 'The Irish are the blacks of Europe, and Dubliners are the blacks of Ireland and North Siders are the blacks of Dublin. So you're black and you're proud of it!' Tentatively they start rehearsals, in a junk room above a billiard parlour, aided and abetted by an old trumpeter who has played with all the greats, and is 'soul' personified. Encouraged by their guru, their manager and a friendly priest who lends them a hall for their first gig, they grow in confidence and technique until conflicting egos bring about their sudden end as a group.

Hardly a revolutionary plot, but a revolutionary film insofar as it shows that your average pleb has it in him or her to knock away the chocks of the welfare state – and fly. And on what better medium than the wings of song? For the Establishment this is a bitter pill to swallow. As long as everyone is down the boozer or slumped in front of the telly, they're happy.

The demise of the group does not mean the end of the story, for if the boys in the band and the girls too can't keep their group together, a few of them soar to greater heights – solo!

The lead singer gets a recording contract and makes it big, another becomes a doctor, another turns to country and western, another forms his own punk metal group, while a duo, less ambitious than the rest, end up busking in the streets, where a lot of the action takes place.

Parker's film is more like a documentary than a feature film, except that the characters are more true to life – funnier, more raucous and randy than the 'real people' seen on your average TV slice-of-life slot. Parker's actors are faultless. Whether they are actually performing or just miming to playback makes no odds.

They look as if they are jamming away at a real live session. The ensemble playing of the group, both on the stage and off, is something to be marvelled at. No one hogs the limelight. Equally charismatic are the people of Dublin, who swarm over the screen. Even the horses are a joy to behold. There is a scene where a broken-down nag stands at the bottom of a tower block, apparently waiting for an elevator. 'You're not taking him up in the lift?' the incredulous Mr Rabbitte asks his minder as the doors slide open. 'I am that,' replies the minder. 'The stairs would kill him.'

If the film has a fault, it lies in Parker's glamorisation of the squalid side of Dublin. He is one of the few directors around who can film dog shit and make it look like hot dogs, which may have something to do with his training in commercials. The pacing of the film is also questionable. The band get too good too quickly, and there are too many similar numbers in the last half hour, when the "yawn" meter on my VCR began to flicker constantly. Gentle pressure on the FF button soon rectified that. Yes, I saw it on my 33-inch Mitsubishi in the sitting room with my B & O 80 Studio Monitors going fit to bust on the 31st of December. What a way to welcome in the New Year! Brilliant! The most innovative musical since *Tommy*!

Tommy started off as a Rock Opera by The Who, about a deaf, dumb and blind boy who finally hears the music, sees the light and sings about it to the whole wide world. Conceived as an album for the group, consisting of Pete Townshend, composer and lead guitarist, John Entwistle, bass guitar, Keith Moon, drums, and Roger Daltrey, lead singer, the work was considerably expanded for the film version. Instruments were added to the score, new numbers were written to flesh out the sketchy plot and various superstars, like Tina Turner, Elton John and Jack Nicholson were recruited to bring their own particular talents to the overall interpretation. Some eggheads turned up their noses at the term 'Rock Opera', but that is what it was, with arias, duets, quartets and choruses. Just like long-haired opera. There were even leitmotivs *à la* Richard Wagner. And it was a good deal more profound than many more pretentious contemporary works by composers like Karlheinz Stockhausen and co.

Tommy's amazing spiritual journey is charted in a series of colourful experiences that leave him shining whiter than white, ripe for religious exploitation. As usual, the disciples become disillusioned and stone their Messiah, who is driven to seek peace in the mountains in his continuing quest for self-awareness. Cue for song. No, not 'Climb Every Mountain' but 'Listening to you I hear the music'. Tommy arrives at the summit in time to meet the rising sun, heralding a new beginning. In South Africa, this image was mistaken as a hymn to paganism, and the entire grand finale was cut out of the film. Pathetic!

If anything, the film is a hymn to pop art, pop culture and pop icons, from pinball tables to Marilyn Monroe, while the episodic nature of the plot, combined with the contrasting musical numbers, produced an overall comic book quality. This was further enhanced by the use of simple dynamic images shot in bold primary colours, for which the production designer Paul Dufficey was largely responsible. The sound was pretty bold too and gave birth to a new term: 'Quintaphonic', which simply added up to three speakers behind the screen and two in the corners at the back of the hall. Woe betide anyone sitting next to one of them. The idea of 'surround sound' as part of a total cinematic experience is fine in theory but there is only one seat in the cinema where it really works and that is the spot where all the sound sources merge into one. If you are at all off centre you'll get an unbalanced sound picture – which is another argument for seeing movies in the home, where stereo and surround sound are fast becoming the norm and you can sit bang in the middle.

CRITIC: Cut the bullshit, Ken. Was *Tommy* a good movie or was it a load of crap?

KEN: (*with Nigel Kennedy accent*) Dunno, mate. Depends if you're into comics 'n Rock 'n Roll, dunnit.

(Normal voice) In many ways *Tommy* was experimental and helped develop the infamous Pop Promo format, pioneered, as I mentioned earlier, by Dick Lester and the Beatles, in the Sixties. I remember these films with affection and, spotting both in a video store the other day, I decided to invest twenty quid in a trip down Penny Lane. *Help!* Money down the drain.

A Hard Day's Night, the Beatles' first effort, was by implication a portrait of the fab four in person. We see them pursued down the streets of Liverpool by a howling mob of teenyboppers, across Lime Street station and on to a London train. During the journey, while they lark about and indulge in fatuous repartee (written by the once fashionable Alun Owen), we are introduced to their manager – as far from Brian Epstein as it is possible to get – and another fictional character, called Grandad. As played by Wilfrid Brambell, with a permanent flasher's leer, he is a monster. For the life of me, I can't fathom what he's doing on the screen. The Beatles, on the other hand, are portrayed as squeaky clean, and, if they rarely utter a sentence longer than four words, not a single four-letter word passes their lips during the entire movie. The plot, which is as slim as George in his neat little mod suit, follows them from home town to the BBC, Lime Street to Lime Grove Studios in London, where they are to appear on a TV variety show. What there is of the plot thickens when Grandad, for no particular reason, winds Ringo up by suggesting he is being exploited by his chums.

The disgruntled drummer then goes walkabout along the Thames, ending up in a cop shop, where he is rescued by his mates just in time for the show. The only time the Beatles and the director let their hair down is when they run wild in a football field to 'Money Can't Buy Me Love'. Shot from the air and also at ground level, this sequence has an exuberance that matches the spirit of the lads themselves and their irresistible music. For the rest, it's everything done to playback in the confines of the studio. The only risqué moment comes when Paul catches Grandad reading a copy of *Queen*, and he turns to the camera saying 'That's an In joke.'

Help! was no joke! Here's the plot. Ringo's life is imperilled by an ancient sacrificial ring stuck on his finger. The ring makes him the target of a group of hilariously demented oriental mystics, who chase the boys from the Swiss Alps to the Bahamas. That's the blurb on the back of the video box and is a pretty fair approximation of the plot – except for the promise of hilarity.

The Goons might have pulled it off as a radio show, but the Beatles were musicians, not madcap comedians. Their hearts don't seem to be in it. There's a silly sequence involving a tank battle on Salisbury Plain where, for no apparent reason, the Beatles are recording a couple of the most unmemorable numbers they ever wrote. A force eight gale is blowing, it's cold, but the fab four do their best to pretend they're having a great time and smile gamely through chattering teeth. In Bermuda, the temperature improves, but the action becomes even more frantic and mirthless.

This was the last feature film the Beatles ever made. I don't wonder. What a wasted opportunity. And yet, back in the Sixties, they seemed funny, didn't they? And wasn't Dick Lester supposed to be a whizz kid? Maybe these harmless romps were 'innocent', but compared with the ribaldry and raw energy of *The Commitments* words like 'commercial', 'mindless' and 'phoney' spring to mind.

In fact the British musical in general has not been much to shout about. The expertise exists, but not the Tin Pan Alley know-how of Hollywood.

I've already exalted the talents of Jessie Matthews, Anna Neagle and Jack Buchanan, even the Beatles. But what of the others – 'The Young Ones' – people like Cliff Richard, who starred in the film of the same name, trying desperately to look interested in a suburban girl with a bouffant hairdo as he serenades her in front of a wire-mesh fence at Ruislip Lido? He doesn't look much happier driving a bus in *Summer Holiday*, or bopping about with Susan Hampshire on a grotty beach in Lanzarote. In *Play it Cool*, Bill Fury jerks around like an epileptic singing to a captive audience of passengers in an aeroplane, while Frankie Vaughan suffers a severe attack of St Vitus in *Those Dangerous Years*. It wasn't until David Essex appeared in *That'll be the Day* and *Stardust* that our pop stars began to get the breaks they deserved, from directors who understood the idiom. These films may have been rough and ready, but they had a style and individuality that owed little to Hollywood.

My first musical mixed both styles together, showing what happens when a big-time Hollywood director takes in a matinée performance of Sandy Wilson's *The Boy Friend*, as staged by a small-time rep company in Portsmouth. Knowing that he is planning his next musical extravaganza and scouting for a star, the cast spend all afternoon upstaging each other. Although it is the self-effacing understudy who finally wins the prize, she elects to stay behind with the Boy Friend, who has helped her through her first show. There are subplots about the petty backstage bitching that I remember from my own touring days in weekly rep, but twelve reels are too long to tell such a slim tale, and Sandy Wilson's music, however tuneful, has diminishing returns, as one pastiche Twenties number follows another.

Despite the big Busby Berkeley routines, the novelty value of the stage show, the great singing and dancing by the cast, which included Twiggy and Tommy Tune, plus the brilliant designs of Shirley Kingdon and Tony Walton, the film was a flop. The acting was too broad, the gags too laboured and the pacing too slow. I should have cut it during the script stage, but, determined to be faithful to the original show, I kept in EVERYTHING! It was left to MGM, who financed the film, to do the job for me. A gorilla in boxing gloves wielding a pair of garden shears could have done a better job.

It's become fashionable these days for some distributors to reissue certain movies like *Blade Runner* and even *The Boy Friend*, in the director's original version, with all the cut material lovingly restored. Whether this heralds a new age of enlightenment is anybody's guess. Maybe the new bosses are smarter than their forefathers, who would cut up their own grandmother to get in four shows a day. A long film meant fewer performances, fewer tickets, fewer peanuts, so nix to long pix. People seem to have wised up. The closer to the director's cut, the better the movie. The better the movie, the better the box office.

Another wide-screen movie musical that started life as a stage show was *Oh What a Lovely War*. The original idea was simplicity itself, and, as performed by Joan Littlewood's talented troupe of players at the Theatre Royal, Stratford, the show was a hit with everyone lucky enough to get tickets. Take a score of World War I pop songs as sung by the long-suffering tommies in the trenches, and you have a bittersweet comment on the folly of war. That was the formula, and it worked. With no more than a dozen or so versatile performers, Joan succeeded in creating the entire British Expeditionary Force from the lowliest private to the loftiest general, as well as the lucky blighters who stayed behind in Blighty.

Sir Richard ('I'm-going-to-attack-the-Establishment-fifty-years-after-it's-dead') Attenborough employed an all-star cast, including four knights and hundreds of extras. He also used dozens of locations, including Brighton Pier – which is not as strange as it first appears when one remembers that Joan's show had a distinct 'end of the pier' flavour. In the film version, the officers conduct the war from this Edwardian Palace of Amusement with a lookout post on top of the Helter Skelter, and the ops room in the ballroom. This is in stark contrast to the cannon fodder, who are shot in the open sewers that were the front line trenches. The two styles don't mix. And the frivolity of the officers alternating with the fatalism of the men soon becomes monotonous.

Nevertheless, the film has telling and imaginative moments, as when a squad of men, stripped to the waist, dig a deep trench as they sing 'I don't want to die, I want to go home'. Cut to GHQ, and the message 'Passchendaele – 244,897' picked out in fairground electric light bulbs. Cut back to the grave piled high with mud as the work squad stand with bowed heads for a moment's silence before they march briskly off singing 'The Bells of Hell go ding-a-ling-a-ling for you, but not for me'.

Another powerful scene is the Sunday church parade among the ruins, with the padre intoning 'Onward, Christian soldiers, March-ing as to war' as the men sing in counterpoint, 'When this lousy war is over'. But perhaps the most poignant sequence is the one that features the sentimental favourite, 'Keep the home fires burning, till the Boys come home', to the accompaniment of an endless procession of stretcher cases draped in blood-red blankets. The men seem to get all the mournful numbers, while the officers, like the devil, have the liveliest tunes.

Caricature, a sense of righteous self-satisfaction, and repetition all undermine the impact of the film, but, for all its faults, *Oh What a Lovely War* has a magnificent ending. Under a cloudless sky a family of bereaved women and children, dressed in summer white, are having a picnic on the South Downs. A group of bare-chested tommies lie sleeping in the lush grass nearby. A newcomer strolls in and joins them. He too lies down and closes his eyes. Then, as the women look towards them, the ghosts of their loved ones slowly dissolve from view. A child asks, 'What did Daddy do in the war, Mummy?' To an infinitely sad rendition of 'They wouldn't believe me', the mother slowly gets up and starts walking down the hill, followed by the others. As we pull away from them, a single white cross comes into shot. The camera rises higher and higher. More and more crosses enter frame – rank upon rank of fallen heroes, regimented in death as they were in life – millions of them stretching up hill and down dale – until the bereaved family become anonymous specks of white, lost among an ocean of white crosses.

For a director not given to poetic flights of fancy, this overwhelming image is a touching memorial to the millions of innocents slaughtered in the Great War.

XVI

Northern Lights

There is a war memorial on Castle Crag, my favourite mini mountain in the Lake District. It is set in Borrowdale stone and commemorates the local lads who died in some foreign field, never to see their beloved valley again, nor mighty Skiddaw, rising in the misty distance like a gigantic bird about to take flight at the far end of Derwent Water. Coleridge called this awe-inspiring mountain 'God made Manifest'. Whether he was on drugs at the time we shall never know, but the Lake District itself acts like a drug to certain sensibilities – my own included. Once hooked, it is hard to kick the habit.

I first visited Cumbria in 1965 in search of the mountain top on which the Pre-Raphaelite artist Dante Gabriel Rossetti had reputedly fought a drunken duel with his mistress – using gin bottles as weapons. Eventually I found the mountain, and made the movie. I also found a little cottage that was to become my home for more than twenty years. The Borrowdale Valley became for me what Monument Valley was for John Ford – a favourite location for every film I made. Though I have to say that the becks, crags, tarns, woods, screes and forces of Borrowdale offer more variety than the sand and stone of Monument Valley.

Magnificent scenery is all very well, but its transference to the screen doesn't necessarily make a magnificent movie, even when it is an integral part of the story. *Swallows and Amazons* is a case in point. I have never read the Arthur Ransome classic but, if it is as dull as the film, I doubt I ever will. The idea of a group of kids on holiday in the Lake District, camping out on an island, has distinct possibilities. But the 1929 dialogue the author puts in the mouths of the children trips uneasily from the tongue, and turns them into little prigs – 'Poor Titty, don't you think that was rather like behaving like a duffer?' Everyone is frightfully prissy and well behaved, never peeing or pooing, and, if they catch a fish, they never do anything as vulgar as gutting and eating it.

A far more realistic picture of camping it up in Lakeland was revealed in *She'll Be Wearing Pink Pyjamas*, which promised less but delivered more. The subject, sensitively directed by John Goldschmidt, dealt with a group of butch dykes (according to a relative) on an outward bound course in the Langdales. They're a mixed bunch of assorted shapes and sizes, mostly feminists, trying to forget the men in their lives by indulging in strenuous exercise and cold showers. But in the dorm, the only subject of conversation is men, men, men. One woman remembers: 'I had sexual inter- course once; neither of us had done it before. We went to a Brighton hotel. He had a book with diagrams. It was awful. I was so ashamed I stole the bedsheets the next morning.'

'Sounds like a case of PCC,' says one sympathetic listener.

'What's that?'

'Post-coital contempt.'

'All the same, I do miss my husband,' says her friend, clamber- ing into a bunk.

'Then try this, love,' she replies, offering her a candle.

From all accounts there was as much fun off the screen as on during the shooting which, uncharacteristically, involved more women than men. Anyone who has ever been involved in filming nude scenes knows how sensitive most artists are to exposing their brightly lit bodies to a crew of fully clothed technicians gawking at them under cover of darkness.

During the filming of *Pink Pyjamas*, the camera crew were approached by a deputation of the female cast involved in an upcoming scene to be shot in the shower room. 'We have been in touch with the actors' union, Equity,' a spokeswoman is reported as saying, 'and they have decreed that in future no female member of the union shall consent to be photographed naked unless all members of the crew working in the immediate vicinity shall likewise appear naked.' So good was the performance of the spokeswoman (I wonder if it was Julie Walters, who was the star of the show) that the gobsmacked technicians fell for it. The sight of the camera crew poised naked around their Arriflex with the lighting cameraman wearing nothing but an exposure meter must have been a memory to treasure!

In *Pink Pyjamas* a generally jaundiced and petty view of life gives way to greater self-awareness and generosity of spirit, as the women become increasingly aware of the recuperative powers of nature on the jaded soul.

On television, it has become commonplace to see some fearsomely bearded mountaineer in trendy climbing gear baring his soul to the viewer, with Everest looming large in the background. It's a pleasant change to watch a bunch of bedraggled women in anoraks struggling up a lowly lakeland fell in the drizzle. Their sense of achievement on reaching the summit is as tangible as the elation experienced by hardened, professional climbers after reaching thirty thousand feet. But, in my experience, women and mountains don't mix. There's *The Sound of Music* of course, but the only female director I know who recognised the significance of the high hills in our lives was Leni Riefenstahl, who made several breathtaking films glorifying mountains before she went on to make a film glorifying Hitler, called *Triumph of the Will*.

Put a man on a mountain with a camera and he produced a BBC documentary; put a woman on a mountain with a camera and she produced the Master Race. Put me on a mountain and I produce art films. *Mahler*, *Song of Summer* (Delius) and *Dante's Inferno* (Rossetti) were all made among the fells of Cumbria which doubled for Bavaria, Norway and Iceland respectively. I also made films on Wordsworth and Coleridge that were set within sight of my front garden and *A British Picture* – an autobiographical film that actually was shot in my front garden – among other local beauty spots that were also immortalised in *The Devils*, *Tommy* and *The Rainbow*. In most of these films the sun shines bright on lake and fell – for the simple reason that I waited for the rain to stop before allowing the cameras to roll.

As any 'outcomer' knows, it rains a lot in the Lake District. One film maker who turned this to his advantage was Bruce Robinson. He rejoiced in the relentless downpour, the more rain the better.

Withnail and I, Bruce's directorial debut, was partly autobiographical. The simple plot follows the efforts of two out-of-work London actors to get away from it all, by taking advantage of Richard Griffiths' offer of a lakeland retreat for a couple of weeks. But the isolated stone cottage is running with damp and the tide of Scottish mist that rolls south across the border resolutely refuses to turn. The wonderful views that surround them never materialise. They are engulfed in a sea of mud and, when the local farmer delivers a load of logs to warm their bones, it turns out to be sodden. It is with some relief that they return to London and the welcome squalor of the flat they abandoned. Stacked with empty bottles, fag ends and piles of dirty plates spawning green slime and fungi, home is the epitome of many a Notting Hill pad I dossed in myself in the Fifties. But, unlike our heroes, I rarely got drunk. If anyone has ever acted a more convincing hangover than Richard E. Grant I have never seen it – and I've seen quite a few. From the fifth row back from the screen in my favourite cinema (The Screen on Baker Street) I caught a whiff of his boozy breath every time he looked my way. In expressing the sheer agony of the alcoholic waiting for the pubs to open, he was painful to watch. I have never felt more anguish for a human being in my life. My favourite Screen has a convenient bar and it is without shame or regret that I recall how I led the stampede at that particular performance.

Bruce caught the flavour of hanging out in the Sixties better than any director I know. He wasn't bad on Cumbria, either.

I, too, finally turned my back on the Lake District. Not because of the rain, though. But when you have an 8.30 call on Hollywood Boulevard it's a long way to commute.

XVII

Hellfire

The Seventies saw the gradual exodus of the American producer from these shores to the promised land – California. Mainly due to government restrictions, it was no longer profitable for them to make films in this country. So, in common with the majority of British directors employed by American companies, I also packed my bags and headed west for a little prospecting. But there are no clear spring mornings in California, no balmy summer days, no glow of autumn, no snap of winter – no roast beef and Yorkshire pudding; just Caesar salad, private swimming pools, endless smog and sunshine. To my surprise, I really missed the rain; and I never settled.

Even so, I made three films in Hollywood – *Altered States*, *Crimes of Passion* and *Whore*. The story behind the last title is ironic. It started life as a play written by a cab driver named David Hines. Moved by the tales told him by fare-paying whores who worked the King's Cross area, he wrote a one-act play called *Bondage*. It received rave notices when it was premiered on the fringe at the Edinburgh Festival. And, one day in London, Hines literally jumped out of his cab and stopped me in the street, to ask if I would write the screenplay; and make it into a film. I read the play and agreed to have a go.

Whore is a tragi-comedy about a British girl on the game at King's Cross. No one in England wanted to know. So I had to go to America for the lolly. Now she's a Hollywood hooker on Sunset Boulevard. So why couldn't I get financed in the UK? The budget was low, the potential high, the risk minimal. Perhaps the subject was considered too sleazy for export. Maybe it could never have been shown on TV. Maybe my face doesn't fit in with the film establishment here. I even had to get all-American money to make three other, very British subjects – all shot in England: *Salome's Last Dance*, *The Rainbow*, and *The Lair of the White Worm*.

Why we are always tripping off to Transylvania in search of Dracula I'll never know. As the same author, Bram Stoker, shows us, in *The Lair of the White Worm*, when it comes to the crunch, you can't beat British incisors. Stoker's creepy tale is set in Derbyshire and, as before, is inspired by vampirism – not with bats and wolves this time, but with worms and the keepers of worms. Just as Dracula is based on a historical figure, so *The Worm* has its roots in historical fact.

My researches led me to the archives of Cecil Sharp House – a treasure-trove of folklore. There I unearthed a folk song which can still be heard of a winter's night in a few Derbyshire pubs today, especially those in the vicinity of Thors Cavern – one of the most impressive caves in England. The song is called 'The Lampton Worm':

> Oh, John Lampton went a fishing once, a fishing in the weir;
> He caught a fish upon his hook that looked almighty queer,
>
> But what the kind of fish it was John Lampton couldn't tell,
> So he took the beastie off the hook and threw it down the well.
>
> Now that worm got fat and growed and growed an awful size
> With great big teeth and a great big mouth and great big goggle
>   eyes;
> And when at night it crawled about a lookin for some booze
> If it felt dry upon the road it milked a dozen cows.
>
> This awful worm would often feed on cows and calves and sheep
> And swallow little babes alive when they lay down to sleep.

So John set out and caught the beast and cut it in two halves
And that soon stopped it eating babes and sheep and calves.

So now you know how all the folks on both sides of the weir
lost lots of sheep and lots of sleep and lived in mortal fear.
So drink the health of brave Sir John who kept the babes from
    harm,
Saved cows and calves by making halves of the famous Lampton
    Worm.

Should you happen to be propping up a bar in Sydney or knocking
back a pint in windy Wellington, you will also hear it ringing in the
rafters, for *The White Worm* became a cult film, appropriately
enough, down under. It did well in other countries, but not in
Merrie England, where our dour-faced critics insisted on taking it
seriously. How on earth can you take seriously the vision of
Catherine Oxenberg, dressed in Marks & Spencer's underwear,
being sacrificed to a fake, phallic worm two hundred feet long?

Another British film which drew upon the darker side of our
heritage, was *The Wicker Man*. Once again, paganism and human
sacrifice are the order of the day.

The action takes place on a remote Scottish island, where a
policeman (Edward Woodward) arrives by flying boat to investi-
gate the disappearance of a teenage girl. From the very start, the
tightknit community gangs up against the outsider, who not only
pokes his nose in where it is not wanted, but also turns out to be a
Protestant prig – as comes to light when he books into the local
pub. Who else would drop to his knees and pray for help in his
winceyette pyjamas, as the landlord's comely daughter, in the
shape of Britt Ekland, rubs her naked body against the adjoining
bedroom wall, slapping her pagan flesh and singing of all the
things she'll give to him? But he prefers to sweat it out alone, and
think of the blessed sacrament. This may save his virtue, but it
doesn't save his life. Wherever his investigations lead, he is

confronted with the old religion: corn dollies in the post office, jars of foreskins in the pharmacy and dancing around the maypole in the playground.

TEACHER: What does this ritual represent?

PUPIL: Please, miss, it represents the penis and the regenerative forces of nature.

How's that for a progressive history lesson? Too far advanced for our prim policeman, who is even further freaked by witnessing a frog being stuffed down a child's throat to take the soreness away. On his way to complain to the local laird, the rectum of this tight-assed cop shrinks even tighter at the sight of a bevy of virgins leaping over a bonfire. When he protests to the laird, played by Christopher Lee in long hair and purple corduroy suit with flares, the latter very sensibly replies – 'Well, you can't jump over fire with your clothes on, can you?'

After a theological debate on the subject 'Does Paganism Pay?', Woodward hurries off through a garden of phallic topiary, waving a paper which authorises him to exhume a grave in which he expects to find the missing girl. He finds a corpse all right, but it is that of a hare. He's already been told that the spirits of dead children enter the bodies of small mammals that gambol in the meadows, so he is not altogether surprised, even though he is miffed at being taken for a fool. Deciding to beat the devious islanders at their own game, he plays the fool himself, by dressing up as Punch during the May Day festivities. The entire population of one hundred and three don animal masks and follow the fool, the hobbyhorse and the man/woman up to the altar, where the missing girl waits to be sacrificed. This act, the Pagans believe, will placate the Gods of Plenty who have been parsimonious with their gifts lately, as one disastrous apple harvest follows another. But in saving the girl, the cop reveals his identity and is quickly overpowered.

Now comes the big revelation. He has been set up. The girl's life was never in danger. She was simply used as bait to lure an outlander into the trap. Woodward turns out to be the one who would fulfil an old prophecy that only a man representing the Queen from across the water could appease the wrath of the Gods. Accordingly, he is stripped of his uniform and pushed into a gigantic wicker basket, in the shape of a man, perched on a hilltop. His cries mingle plaintively with the squawks of assorted poultry, doomed like himself to a good roasting. As the blood-red sun sets, the victim impotently rattles the bars of his wooden cage. A flaming torch sets the primitive giant alight. The Islanders link hands and dance around it, while the laird declaims: 'Death to you will bring rebirth to our crops.' But the barbecuing policeman, game to the last, shouts back amid roaring flames. 'If you kill me now, it is I who will live again, not your damned apples. For I believe in the life eternal. There is no Sun God! Killing me is not going to bring back your apples. Awake, you heathens (*cough, cough*), it is the Lord who has laid waste your orchards.'

By now the Wicker Man is a towering inferno. But, as the encircling Pagans chant 'Summer is a comin' in', the voice of the true believer is heard to shout, 'The Lord is my shepherd; I shall not want,' before his final cry is taken up by the seagulls.

The sun sinks slowly in the west, yet again, and the credits begin to roll on one of the strangest films ever made on these shores. The fact that it is curiously moving is paradoxical. The photography is mundane, and the acting by the professionals only a cut above that of the islanders, which is understandably amateurish. The natives treat the whole thing like a game, which, of course it is. So that sort of works. And the island itself casts a spell of its own upon the proceedings. Lastly, there is the performance of Edward Woodward as the duped policeman, which can only be described as dogged. It's as though he discovered on day one that he was mixed up with a potential disaster, but decided that come hell or high water he would give the part his best shot.

I don't know whether Anthony Shaffer was trying to write a horror movie or a black comedy. Either way, *The Wicker Man* is genuinely disturbing. We still don't know the truth about what happened in the Orkney Islands only a short time ago. The suspicion that it could actually happen makes *The Wicker Man* linger in the mind, long after more polished horror movies have faded from memory.

Another rough and ready horror film that sticks in the mind is *Hellraiser*, which started a new genre known as 'Vamporn'. A vamp lures men to her home, where she brutally murders them, in order that her skinless, half-decomposed boyfriend Frank may eventually achieve rejuvenation by sucking their blood. So where's the porn? Well, that pops up throughout the film like a running gag that makes you want to gag. It starts the moment a hundred fish-hooks pierce Frank's naked flesh and tear him apart in a shower of blood. And it is blood that brings him back to life, long after his corpse has been stuffed under the floorboards.

His brother, Larry, takes over the deserted property ten years later. While attempting to put the place in order, he catches his hand on a nail. And, as the blood drip, drip, drips on to the bare boards that absorb it like blotting paper, so do the grisly remains below. Larry, alarmed about his cut, observes none of this as he dashes off for a bandage. Iron nails rise steaming out of trembling floorboards, rats scamper, and putrefying liquid oozes from the cracks, which widen as the floor splits apart to reveal two dripping, skeletal limbs that shoot up out of the slime, followed by a glutinous, skull-less brain. Skinless fingers follow, as Frank's repulsive remains arise agonisingly from their wooden tomb.

We know it is all special effects and UB-40, but that doesn't make the spectacle any less nauseating. The victim's tormentors are obscene. Garbed in black rubber – Dick head, Pin head and Clit head, so called for obvious reasons, make a very unholy trinity. Known as Cenobites, they appear from a mysterious Pandora's Box acquired by their victim in the Far East. Opening the intricate lid conjures them from the pit. They promise experience beyond the limit, and that's exactly where Mr Barker goes.

His follow-up, *Hellbound*, was even more revolting. When a slippery, slimy, monstrous abortion materialised from a putrid mattress, for a moment I was reminded of a canvas by Francis Bacon, but his imagery is like Disney when compared with Barker's.

Blood is also heavily featured in one of the most ingenious horror films I have ever seen. Aptly enough it was called *Theatre of Blood* – and it was British. The plot couldn't be simpler. A group of heartless critics drive an actor named Lionheart to suicide, and he returns from beyond the grave to exact a terrible revenge. As they are murdered one by one, we see that, like the Lord High Executioner in *The Mikado*, Lionheart makes the punishment fit the crime.

For instance, a critic who buried him for a bad performance of Julius Caesar is stabbed to death during the Ides of March. Then, disguised as a gravedigger, Lionheart comes to bury him. As his fellow critics mourn his loss around the grave, a horse gallops up, dragging the corpse of the critic who gave Lionheart a murderous review in *Troilus and Cressida*.

> Come, tie his body to my horse's tail;
> along the field I will the Trojan trail.

For a bad notice of *Cymbeline*, in which Imogen wakes up to find her husband's severed head beside her, the offending critic and his wife suffer the same fate.

Another vitriolic critic, who slept through Lionheart's *Richard*

III in a drunken stupor, is drowned in a tub of malmsey at a wine tasting. 'I wonder if he'll travel well?' muses Lionheart, as he hammers down the lid.

But the most fitting punishment of all is reserved for Robert Morley, who plays a terrible old pouf in a pink suit. He concocts a tasteless review for Lionheart's performance in *Titus Andronicus*, in which a queen is made to eat her children baked in a pie. Our critical queen has two white pouffy poodles which he calls his babies. So when he finally discovers that the delectable dish he is devouring is really poodle *à la crème* he goes to throw up – only to have a funnel rammed down his throat, followed by even more indigestible poodle. 'Pity he didn't have the stomach for it,' murmurs the avenged thespian.

Vincent Price, as the fallen star, and Diana Rigg, the daughter who colludes in his crimes, are exceptionally good. Ian Hendry, Coral Browne, Arthur Lowe, Robert Morley, Michael Hordern and Jack Hawkins, as the critics, all deserve glowing reviews. And so do director Douglas Hickox and writer Anthony Greville-Bell. Also deserving of praise are the crowd of winos and dropouts who save Lionheart from a watery grave after his suicidal plunge into the Thames. They become a raggle-taggle troupe of extras who help Vincent Price perform his elaborate revenge.

Two names sprang out of the list of talented players, as end credits rolled after the spectacular finale in which Lionheart plunges to his doom in a blazing theatre. The names that made me sit up were Sally Gilmore and John Gilpin. There was a time when these two names would draw crowds to that very theatre, deserted and dust-covered in the film, which used to ring with applause nightly in the late Forties, when I was an enthusiastic balletomane. Gilmore and Gilpin were the two brightest stars of the Ballet Rambert. *The Mermaid, Dark Elegies, Lilac Garden, The Judgement of Paris*, and *Lady into Fox* were pure magic. *The Mermaid* featured Sally in the title role, with John Gilpin as the shipwrecked mariner who falls in love with her. Everyone was in love with Sally in those days. It never occurred to me that she would ever grow old. She reminded me of Alice in Wonderland. Blond John Gilpin also epitomised eternal youth. The two of them were luminaries of the dance, who never failed to impart a warm glow to the audience whenever they appeared. Strange to see them looking ugly and depraved in the same surroundings, a quarter of a century later. Meaningless names to most punters watching the movie – but still in there, giving their all as they probably have done all their working lives.

It was in the same theatre I saw Donald Wolfit doing his best with the Bard. I wonder if Lionheart, with his hammy gestures and booming tones, was based on that extraordinary actor who, regardless of the size of the audience, always gave of his very best.

But critics rarely give good marks for effort. By and large they are a bigoted lot, and in *Theatre of Blood* they received their just reward. Criticism has become a blood sport. It makes a refreshing change to see the hunters hunted down instead of the hapless quarry.

Having been pursued for years by unspeakable reviewers, perhaps I have developed a taste for blood myself, and have been guilty of savaging the occasional sacred cow too violently. But perhaps sacred cows are fair game. And, as Lionheart says to one critic he is about to do away with, 'How many artists have you killed because you lacked the ability to create yourself?'

This is probably as good a moment as any to explain why I may not have mentioned your favourite movie or director – yet. Don't fret, there's still another couple of chapters to go, and this guided tour down the highways and byways of the British film scene was planned not only to include great monuments, like Canterbury Cathedral, but also places like the slums of Nine Elms and the stone cottages of Cumbria, not to mention the occasional flight of fancy in foreign climes. And there's not time to see everything. That's another trip.

Previous page: Lawrence of Arabia and friend

Left: The Emerald Forest

Right: Homage to Busby Berkeley in Portsmouth. *The Boy Friend*

Left: The Kitchen Toto

Right: Homage to Soul in Dublin. *The Commitments*

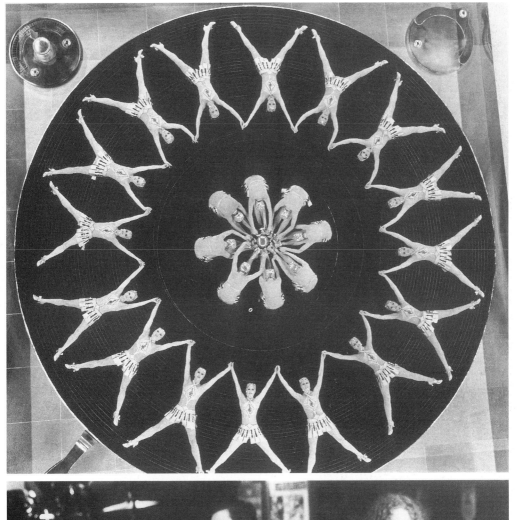

Left: Fun in
Lakeland.
*Swallows and
Amazons*

Right: Hell in
Lakeland.
Withnail and I

Left: She'll Be
Wearing Pink
Pyjamas

Right: Oh! What
a Lovely
Graveyard

The Wicker Man

Below: Lair of the White Worm

Foot: The 39 Steps

Left: Get Carter

Below: Frenzy

Leon, the Pigfarmer

Kenneth's friends in *Peter's Friends*

XVIII

Thriller

The mention of dead cows reminds me of one of the oddest British thrillers ever made – *The Long Good Friday*. In what was one of his first starring roles, Bob Hoskins plays an East End gangland boss bent on discovering who is responsible for blowing up his Rolls, his pub and his casino. In an effort to make any potential suspect talk, he has his boys round up every crook in town and hang them upside down, like sides of beef, on meat hooks suspended from a moving chain that transports them into the warehouse's refrigeration unit. There he offers them a deal.

'Frostbite or verbals!'

Although all turn as bright as beetroots, no one confesses, because no one did it.

Later, after a good deal of blood-letting, it transpires that the IRA are responsible, getting their own back over a shady construction deal pulled by one of Bob's mob when his boss was out of town. Out of his depth against this lot, Hoskins finally is taken for a ride from which there will be no return. The film is laced with mordant humour. Bob even lectures the New York Mafia on their dated image. He plans to take his business into Europe, where Britain's future is. So he died a true patriot and Thatcherite. The only disappointment in this criminal carry-on is Helen Mirren, as the gangster's moll. With her West End accent, she looks far from comfortable curled up on a divan with East End Bob. I heard that she wasn't entirely happy with a purely decorative role and wanted to tote a machine gun. In which case, the IRA might have met their match. I haven't seen any other films by John Mackenzie. He's hot on fireworks and atmosphere, but a bit of a damp squib when it comes to storytelling.

Mike Hodges has had an uneven career in the cinema, but he made a cracking good movie about the Newcastle Mafia with *Get Carter*. This thriller featured Michael Caine as a small-time crook who sees his brother's young daughter in a porno film and starts a personal vendetta against all those involved. It's a dirty film set in a dirty city. The director exploits his dramatic locations to the full. Some of the scenes are almost surrealistic, as when Caine comes out of a house stark naked, and falls into step with an all-girl Kazoo band marching along in kilts.

There is an exciting car chase that is the equal of any of the spectacular American ones we are always seeing in San Francisco – which, in a slag-bag sort of way, Newcastle resembles. And, as Carter combs this grotty universe to get the corrupters of youth, they set out to get Carter. One victim of the vendetta goes to her death in a car boot, headed for the bottom of the Tyne, while the last but one is bumped off by a travelling bucket on to a slag heap. And Caine himself is picked off by a sniper's bullet that sends him sprawling into a coal-sodden sea.

It is a shame we don't see more of provincial England in the movies but, as I've said before, it's all a question of economics. Living allowances can burn up a third of your budget. If you are filming less than fifty miles from home, those expenses don't apply, which is a very good reason why films on London's underworld are still an attractive proposition, especially if they are based on real, live criminals as in *The Krays*. Actually, *The Craze* might have been a better title, if Peter Medak's film has any claims to authenticity!

We first see these terrible twins as cuddly babes at their christening, then as schoolboys living in the East End during the Blitz, where Grandad entertains them in the air raid shelter with bedtime stories about Jack the Ripper.

No sooner are the boys grown up than they buy a couple of cutlasses, and start carving people up with the same relish that others might use to attack the Sunday joint. But, for all their misanthropy, they love their Mum. In fact, the last shot in the picture shows them standing at her graveside – handcuffed. This is the first time we see any evidence that the law exists. Although the brothers indulge in GBH wherever they go and even machine-gun a gang of Maltese hoods, the boys in blue are always conspicuous by their absence. But this makes a change from the contemporary cliché of endless police corruption.

Right at the beginning, however, we are treated to the spectacle of a comic representative of the law, who pedals up to the family home wearing a steel helmet and looking for Dad, who is fast asleep as usual. For a moment, Mum stops her moaning (she's a great moaner, is Mum), wakes Dad up and hides him under the stairs, which is the last place the dumb officer thinks of looking. Panic over, as he pedals out of the picture, leaving a puzzled audience behind him. What is Dad's crime – apart from his inability to keep awake? He looks too old to fight.

This is the first mystery of many. Throughout the film, un-savoury characters come and go, mouthing threats and obsceni-ties. They are awarded great chunks of screen time, but who they are and what they are up to is never revealed. Neither is the Krays' rise to fame properly chronicled. A promising liaison with an American gang is dropped as soon as it starts. And this style of film-making went out of fashion with those Edgar Wallace movies of the Thirties. So you might wonder why I'm wasting space on it.

The answer lies in the personalities of the brothers playing the brothers. I am speaking of Gary and Martin Kemp, who im-personate Ron and Reg. I believe they are pop stars. Even so, they are totally convincing, although neither looks strong enough to knock the skin off a rice pudding. They have menace, they have arrogance, they have style. It would be tempting to say they were simply playing themselves. On the other hand, it could also be great acting. Who knows? The fact that they are fresh to the screen, and do not come to their parts dragging tried and tested acting techniques behind them, like the rest of the cast, has to be a bonus. It seems that we have heard Billie Whitelaw whingeing on as a working-class mum for decades, although 'Take your fingers out of your Dad's nose! There's germs up there,' must be a new line, even for her.

Twins from a broken family, dominated by women, they both suffer from an Oedipus complex. But whereas Reg is straight, Ron is bent. Inflamed with jealousy when Reg marries a blonde, Ron becomes increasingly paranoid and sadistic. Reg's wife doesn't find that marriage is all it's cracked up to be, and takes her own life. For a while Reg is inconsolable, until his brother gives him a pep talk. This snaps Ron out of it and the two lads go off to celebrate. Reg shoots a man in the head at point-blank range, while Ron stabs an old man in the eye, and goes on and on stabbing him until the living-room carpet is a pool of blood. Mum goes on watching telly.

Then we're in the cemetery and on to the subtitles informing us of the whereabouts of the terrible twins – in case we should like to visit them, I suppose. Why only one is in Broadmoor I cannot imagine. Can their pathological behaviour be the result of those bloody tales about Jack the Ripper in the underground station? Those temporary air raid shelters were pretty scary places, according to one female member of the Kray Clan, who remembers helping to assist a woman in labour. 'I had to cut the baby's head off to save the woman's life. But it was no good, she died too.' She then goes into a diatribe about women having abortions while men enjoy themselves playing at war. And she winds up saying, 'They stay kids all their fucking lives, but women have to grow up and they become victims.' Whereupon she coughs up blood and pegs out in the next scene. Not before time. What with mother Kray threatening to slit her husband's throat in front of the children –

well, I mean, it's hardly setting a good example to us boys, is it? No wonder we turn out rotten. And that is the moral of the tale, I suppose. At least their brutal natures can't be blamed on too much telly. They only had steam radio when the Krays were kids, where the most violent programme they were likely to hear was the nightly serial 'Dick Barton, Special Agent' – which came shortly after 'Childrens' Hour'.

As far as the film is concerned, the director is to be commended for his restraint. For I understand that the Krays used to stick their victims' fingers into electric sockets, while whipping them with barbed wire. Possibly Peter Medak is saving it for *Krays II*. If this happens, I hope he gets his London looking more like London this time, and not like the set we last saw on the Elstree lot in *Passport to Pimlico*. Medak's sojourn in Hollywood seems to have affected his ability to create the London we love.

The same could be said for another director of thrillers, probably the greatest director of them all – Alfred Hitchcock.

Whereas Medak was hampered by having to create a London of the past in a London of the present, Hitchcock, who was born and bred here, had no such excuse in *Frenzy*, which was a contemporary subject. But then he had been away in Lotus Land even longer than Medak.

Aerial shots of the capital, accompanied by bright music, compensating for the dull weather, lead us to the Thames, in which a sex doll is floating. At least it looks like a sex doll. But from the remarks of the onlookers, it becomes clear that the dummy is a dead woman dressed in nothing but a necktie, fastened a little too tight for comfort. 'Rapes 'em first, don't 'e?' says one rubbernecking tart to another. 'Nice to know every cloud 'as a silver lining,' comes the sick reply.

From this moment on, the dialogue slides into a Thirties time warp around the era of Hitch's *The 39 Steps*. Here's a sample from a cockney maid: 'With all the evidence against 'im they'd lock 'im up without as much as a by-your-leave, cross me 'art and 'ope t'die.' But if some of the dialogue is as heavy as a blunt instrument, Hitch's sense of visual comedy is razor sharp. The killer has to retrieve an incriminating piece of evidence from one of his victims. The crucial item is a tiepin, decorated with the killer's initials, which was grasped by the strangled woman during her frantic death struggle. The murderer only realises this some time after he has disposed of the body on the back of an open lorry at Covent Garden market – in a sack of potatoes. Under cover of darkness, he climbs back on the lorry – just in time to bury himself among the bulging sacks as it unexpectedly sets off. As the rickety vehicle roars up the M1, the killer has to worm his way into the sack of cascading potatoes and claw his way up the corpse. Imagine his horror when he finds that rigor mortis has set in, and there is only one way to retrieve the tiepin. The crack of her finger joints breaking one by one sends shivers up the spine even now.

Technically *Frenzy* is a mess, and if an editor of Jimmy Jympson's stature is unable to smooth out the bumpy narrative, then no one can. I seem to remember him telling me that Hitch was ill at the time. Even so, something remains of the master's touch, displayed so magically in *The 39 Steps*. Any rough edges here can be attributed to the impetuosity of youth rather than the infirmity of old age.

We open in a music hall – presumably in the East End, for all the members of the audience haranguing the Man with the Incredible Memory on stage have broad 'Cor blimey, Lor luvyer' cockney accents. Standing out from the rest of the house is a tailor's dummy, who asks the sage how far it is from Winnipeg to Manitoba or somewhere. After a few more tedious questions and answers a shot is fired, and the extras stampede for the exit.

In the studio street outside, the tailor's dummy, who turns out to be none other than debonair Robert Donat, is accosted by a short woman with a foreign accent and a saucy hat. She asks to go home with him. Being a perfect gentleman, he tips his Homburg and offers his arm.

Once in his flat, the mysterious woman tells him to turn the lights out and she says she's hungry. Donat graciously fries her a kipper, still in his overcoat with a fag in his mouth. But the meal goes cold when he finds her sprawled across his bed, murmuring, 'Clear out, Hannay, they'll get you next.' Noting the knife deeply embedded in her back, he needs no further encouragement.

The scream of the landlady when she finds the body segues neatly into the shrill whistle of the train bearing our hero to the Highlands. In his carriage Hannay buries himself in his seat as he recognises his picture on the front page of a newspaper, and realises that he is wanted for murder. The frivolous chat of two 'travellers' in ladies' underwear discussing their product wittily emphasises Hannay's growing distress. Then he is recognised by a bobby in Glasgow as he changes trains and the chase is on. The police are coming down the corridor. He enters a compartment occupied by a beautiful blonde. He throws himself into her arms like a long-lost lover. But she is not having any and denounces him, whereupon he jumps out of the window, lands on the Forth Bridge and makes his escape.

How he ends up handcuffed to the blonde and running through the heather that very same night, pursued not only by the police but also by the baddies, has to be seen to be believed. So let's cut to the pub bedroom where Hannay and the reluctant blonde spend the night. There's a delicious moment of comic eroticism when the blonde removes her wet stockings, while Hannay eats a sandwich. Naturally his hand has to go where her hand goes – and so does the camera.

Suave playing by Donat and Madeleine Carroll make for a super comedy thriller. They could have made a great comedy team, although rumour has it that they hated each other and that during filming Hitch accidentally on purpose lost the key to the handcuffs.

It was bad enough that the couple had to take lunch together, but absolute hell when they had to go to the loo.

The two remakes I have seen of *The 39 Steps* pale into insignificance compared with the original. Film techniques may have improved, but who cares a fig about that? If films were judged only by their technical excellence, who would remember master-pieces like Fellini's *La Strada* or Jean Vigo's *L'Atalante*?

XIX

The End?

And what about future masterpieces of British cinema? Hardly a week goes by without a journalist or TV researcher telephoning to ask my opinion about the future of the British film industry. What is it? What happened to it? Gainsborough, Riverside and Ealing Studios were bought by the BBC. There's the short answer. The film industry was swallowed up by TV. The film industry is not dead, but merely flourishing. More feature-length films are being made in Great Britain than ever before. They are all destined for the small screen, but many have a life in cinemas throughout the world.

A case in point is my last film, *Lady Chatterley* – based on three related novels by D. H. Lawrence. This was a co-production between London Films (Alexander Korda's old company), Global Arts (a predominantly Italian group) and BBC Films. Two feature-film interests and one television – a tripart association that is fast becoming the norm.

The film was shot on 35 mm and starred Joely Richardson and Sean Bean. The result was first seen on BBC television in four 50-minute episodes – which made me very happy. It's not every day that a director has the opportunity to bring a great novel to the screen in its entirety. That was my problem with *Women in Love*. It was impossible to do justice to the 600-page original in 120 minutes of screen time. An extra 80 minutes would have made all the difference.

So your 'cut down' feature-film version of *Lady Chatterley* must be a compromise, I hear you say. It's a different film, certainly, and moves at a different pace. With a break of one week between each TV episode one can afford a more leisurely approach, even a certain amount of repetition, and Lawrence is a great one for repetition. When it came to editing down all the material for the feature-film version I was spoilt for choice. Strangely enough, the sequences of scenes in my final cut were not the ones that worked best on paper, and they were not necessarily assembled in the same order or even at the same length as they appeared in the TV version. With film, you can remould and reshape your material, as a sculptor models his clay, and always come up with something fresh and exciting, and maybe have a few laughs on the way, even when things look black.

There was a particular incident in *Lady Chatterley* involving Mellors' dog. In the book she's called Flossie, but our black labrador was called Bramble and would only answer to that name, so the gamekeeper's dog had to be rechristened. But she was a lazy bitch, and often her mother and sister were called upon as substitutes. They looked identical and also answered to the name of Bramble. The animal handler left nothing to chance, and it was through no fault of her own that she and her dogs failed to turn up for filming one morning. There had been a mistake on the call sheet, with the result that Bramble was not around to complete a scene that had been left over from the previous day. So there was Lady Chatterley standing in the middle of her stately hallway and there was Mellors standing opposite her, discussing Bramble – who should have been lying on the floor between them. Consternation. Excuses and explanations, but no Bramble – at least for the three hours it would take the handler and her Brambles to jump into the Landrover and drive over. What to do, with £250 per minute ticking away on the clock? Brainwave – didn't the wardrobe boy have a black Labrador? Yes, he was always playing ball with it during the lunchbreak. But it was untrained and only answered to the name of Jock. If we didn't start shooting soon, we'd be behind schedule and over budget.

So, despite our continuity girl's cries of horror, the scene that started with an overweight Labrador bitch lumbering into shot ended with a lithe Labrador pup bounding out of shot with balls bouncing. The only thing the animals had in common was their breed and their colour. But, as the producer remarked philosophically, as we got back on schedule, 'Well, if the audience are clocking a dog's bollocks instead of the actors, then we should recast.'

'That was the swiftest sex change in history,' commented the continuity girl. She wasn't really worried, because she knew that no one would notice such an error on the television. As for the wide screen, I'm not so sure. Heck! Small screen, wide screen, I'm sick of the attitude that presupposes that if a film is made for the big screen it must be better. I've seen several dual-purpose movies of late on a variety of screens both glass and plastic, and I doubt if the choice affected my appreciation one jot.

It has to be admitted that the cinema screen enhances the 'grain', making the viewer conscious of the deficiencies of the stock on which the image is photographed. With television, the image is not only small but focused on glass, which gives it a greater luminosity. In other words, it is more lifelike. One is also viewing the picture on the centre axis so there is no distortion, which is not the case from a seat on the side in a cinema where the reflected image is relatively dim. As all the prints shown on TV are mint copies, there are no scratches to distract us and the picture is never out of focus. By and large, the TV presentation of a movie, in Nicam stereo with surround sound, has the cinema – with all its attendant costs and general inconveniences – beat by a mile.

Another point in favour of the dual feature/TV movie is that it gives untried talent a real chance to prove its worth. This was simply not possible in the days of the feature-film system, with its rigid hierarchies and old boy network. And the subject matter on offer today is far wider-ranging than in the past.

A case in point is *The Bridge*, adapted from a novel by Maggie Hemingway and directed by Syd Macartney – a name new to me. A subtitle, which I hope I've got right, quickly puts us in the picture: 'The story is inspired by the impressionist painter Wilson Steer. He visited Suffolk regularly as a young artist. Everything else in the film is speculation.'

What follows is a classic tale of an artist falling in love with his model, who, in this case, happens to be a respectable married woman with a family. There are also footnotes on the nature of art and the power of inspiration.

On the first day of his annual holiday, Wilson Steer, a present-able youth in a straw hat, awakens from a nap on the beach to see a vision on top of a sand dune. It is a trim Edwardian lady with a parasol, attired in white from head to toe. A moment later she reacts to a shout from one of her children, and disappears.

From that blinding moment, Steer becomes obsessed with the woman, and engineers a meeting during which he talks her into posing for him. Isabel doesn't need much persuading, as she is immensely attracted to this handsome stranger. The victim of a loveless marriage, with her husband away much of the time on business, she is ripe for seduction. But, being an honourable woman and a dutiful wife, Isabel is consumed with guilt by her feelings, and is unable to relax with the young artist.

'I'm sorry, it's hopeless,' he says, throwing down his brush. 'The truth is, we've already done the sitting. Dozing on the beach, I woke up and there you were. It's just a question of painting what I saw. I have to paint to show the way I feel.'

'You must feel passionately about your subjects,' she says, eyeing the canvas.

'Some more than others,' he replies pointedly.

That same evening they meet at the local fête, in which some of her children are participating. Steer dances with Emma, one of Isabel's young daughters, then joins Mum among the spectators. They sit, side by side, staring straight ahead in silence, watching an interminable series of historical tableaux. The feeling of intimacy between them grows stronger every second, as Prince Albert proposes to Victoria, Queen Elizabeth knights Sir Walter Raleigh and the Indians mutiny. Cannons fire. They finally look at each other full in the face. Fireworks! The silence is broken. They enjoy the pyrotechnics and talk.

'I've had an invitation to join friends in France,' says Steer.

'I thought you were going to spend summer near here,' says Isabel. 'Emma will be heartbroken!'

'Always Emma,' snaps Steer.

'Not just Emma,' replies Isabel.

They hold hands in silence until it is time to leave, when Steer carries the sleeping Emma home in his arms. So ends one of the most emotionally charged moments I have seen on the screen for ages. Their mutual passion, held in check by the conventions of the day, was painful to behold.

Not wishing to put Isabel's marriage under further strain, Steer goes to France, eschewing all temptation to commit the local scenery to canvas in favour of working on his portrait of the Lady in White. When it is finished, Steer cannot bear his separation from Isabel a moment longer, and returns to Suffolk, where their dream of love is consummated.

The husband sees the finished portrait and guesses the truth. Bribes and threats of suicide follow, with the distraught Isabel rushing down to a footbridge which crosses a river near the estuary. From a distance, Steer watches the husband talk his errant wife out of any rash act that might destroy the family. This scene also proves to be a potent image for Steer and, at another time and another place, he is seen immortalising it for posterity. But this is not art. It is reportage. So Steer wipes the canvas clean and starts again. The finished work, one of this painter's most compelling canvases, shows the man and the woman on the bridge – transfigured! Now they are relaxed figures in a landscape, not tense protagonists in a domestic drama. They both wear hats now and look like a couple out for a Sunday stroll, who have paused for a moment to admire the view. An air of tranquillity emanates from the canvas, as does the soft warmth of a sunny afternoon in Suffolk where, as Steer mentioned with some relish at the start of his holiday, 'Nothing ever happens'.

So ends a touching story, which also illustrates how a personal experience can be transformed into a work of art with wide appeal. But how wide? Will *The Bridge* go down well abroad, you may ask? Will it win international prizes? Will it be a commercial hit in Japan? Will it do well in the Midwest? Will it mean anything to a cab driver in Holboken, New Jersey? I don't know and, what is more, I don't care. It's a sensitive, well-made film, to be enjoyed by anyone who believes in old-fashioned values. If that rules out the majority of the 'under thirty-fives' who make up ninety per cent of the cinema-going audience today, that's tough! They've got *Lethal Weapon 1, 2* and *3* to blow them away.

As long as the investors don't get their fingers burnt, the chances are that many more films like *The Bridge* will continue to be made here, and be appreciated, like *Enchanted April*, yet another stylish and compassionate study of the repressed British housewife ripe for adventure.

Italy rather than Suffolk proves to be the liberating factor here, and, if the film doesn't quite capture the enchantment of the novel from which it was adapted, this did not prevent it from capturing three Oscar nominations.

There is a tendency for these charming trifles to go on a bit. They are low on excitement, share a uniformity of style and are short on cinematic flair. The acting is generally as subdued as the screenplay demands, the photography self-effacing and the art direction respectable, while the period clothes look as if they had been supplied by the same theatrical costumier – which is invariably the case.

But not all Screen 2 or Screen 4 co-productions are steeped in our glorious past. Contemporary subjects, often by new directors, are also very much in evidence. But they tend to be less successful. One notable exception was *Truly, Madly, Deeply*, which was a big box office hit in the cinema before it was transmitted on TV.

This is the story of a girl in love with a ghost. Bereft when her lover ups and dies, she moves into a new place to try to get him out of her system and start life afresh. But, despite a trio of lovesick workmen putting her house in order, the poor girl just can't cope. Even her analyst can't help. So it's left to the inamorato to come back from the grave and fuck some sense into her. He also bosses her about and brings a band of ghosts into her bedroom to play Bach all night long. That does it. She cuts him dead and takes up with the first man she bumps into, who happens to be a vastly unattractive art-therapy teacher with whom, presumably, she lives happily ever after.

Predictably, the critics loved it – truly, madly and very deeply. They praised the performance of Juliet Stevenson, as the necrophiliac, to the skies. Aye, there's the rub! That's what it was – a performance – a word often associated with seals balancing balls on their noses. What they do is clever, but you couldn't call it acting. There were several occasions when I almost expected Ms Stevenson to pat herself on the back for being so clever. Every blink of an eye, tilt of the chin, twitch of the nose seem choreographed to the demands of the script. I didn't catch one moment of honest emotion. The ghost of Alan Rickman was far more real. Even so, I don't buy it. Reality and fantasy seldom mix.

It all left me as cold as a dead man's dick – which reminds me of another co-production – Peter Greenaway's *Drowning by Numbers*.

What is it about Greenaway's films that makes the flesh crawl? I think it's his apparent loathing of the human race. Unable to watch the humiliating spectacle of that fine actor, Bryan Pringle, cavorting drunk and naked in a tin bath in what must be the worst performance of his career, I switched channels. An hour or so later I switched back, to see if he'd sobered up, to find a chubby, ten-year-old boy sitting up naked in bed, surrounded by bloodstained sheets. I seem to remember two alarmed women entering the room, and asking what had happened. 'I've circumcised myself,' replied the boy, 'with a pair of scissors.' Is this gross, or is this gross?

I remember Michael Nyman, who composes most of Greenaway's film scores, telling me that he usually supplies the director with reams of music, not necessarily composed for any particular scene, which Greenaway cuts into arbitrary chunks according to his needs. It seems to me that Greenaway treats the human race in much the same way. And he is more interested in shit than soul.

Another trendy writer/director, with a self-conscious style and a habit of distancing himself from his subjects, is the self-obsessed Terence Davies. The moment I saw 'The British Film Institute in association with Channel 4 presents *Distant Voices, Still Lives*' I feared we were in for a downer, and so it proved. There followed a slice of nostalgia as brown as a Hovis loaf. Told mostly in a series of static set-ups in and around the family home in a provincial town during the last war, this snapshot album of a film chronicles the fortunes of a family dominated by a near homicidal maniac.

Someone told me that this monster of depravity, who sweeps the Christmas dinner off the table on to the floor, punches his wife in the face and wallops the kids for getting caught in an air raid, was actually the director's father. If this is so, and Mr Davies is trying to exorcise this brute from his psyche, then he should see an analyst, and not inflict his therapy on us.

For much of the film Davies' camera is locked off, as in the very early days of the Biograph, where the camera stays clamped to its tripod on the station platform, filming miles of empty track before the train finally comes into shot. I believe Mr Davies went to film school – presumably not for long.

Dead Again, made in Hollywood, was evidence that Kenneth Branagh is alive and kicking. But *Peter's Friends* doesn't exactly pulsate with passion or flair. Known in the trade as *Kenneth's Friends*, this film resurrects the weekend house party, beloved of Agatha Christie and Noel Coward. I used the same idea in *Gothic*, which was actually shot in the same house, as was my last film, *Lady Chatterley*. No, I don't own it or rent it out. I wish I did. I'd have retired years ago. It just happens to be one of the very few stately homes not owned by the National Trust, who seem more interested in entertaining tourists with cream teas than film units with lethal weapons.

I recall an incident which occurred at Wrotham Park during the making of *Gothic*. We were filming a duel between Byron's biographer, Polidori, and the poet Shelley. The fight, which took place in the dining room, ended with Shelley flicking his opponent's rapier out of his grasp and on to the floor. For five takes it all worked perfectly, but take six, which proved to be the last, ended with the rapier flying through the air and embedding itself in a priceless Gainsborough. My first thought was that this sort of thing only happened in *Tom & Jerry* cartoons. My second was that the owner would chuck us out of the house directly he heard the news. Not wanting to prolong the agony, I sought out Mr Byng in the billiard room, where he was punishing a pair of ivory balls. He looked grave as I stammered out my implausible tale, concluding with a pathetic, 'Sorry'.

'Describe the painting to me,' he said flatly.

I did so.

'Thank God,' he said, giving me a friendly pat on the shoulder. 'It's only the second-best Gainsborough.'

We won a reprieve. When the next accident occurred, several years later, we knocked his stately wrought-iron gates off their stately hinges with a two-thousand-kilowatt genny. Mr Byng was abroad, and we were able to fix them before his return.

I wonder if Kenneth Branagh had any similar problems while filming his house party, which avoids the Agatha Christie device of serving up a succession of corpses. That's not to say that the protagonists don't feel like murdering each other at times. The guests are all old mates who came down from university together ten years ago, and have not met again as a group until now, when one of their number comes into his inheritance and invites his chums to help him celebrate and bring in the New Year at the same time. They're all changed out of recognition, and end up hating each other until their host, Peter, reveals that he has AIDS, whereupon they all become terribly sympathetic and live happily ever after, including Peter, who's destined to die in the arms of his ever-loving nanny.

Not a very original idea. Could be good, could be bad. Depends on the cast and the script. Promising cast. What of the script? I could see them writing it. Oh, let's have one of the men – Peter's best friend – as a writer who has sold out to Hollywood, and married an American TV soap star who is obsessed with her body – an aerobics freak and compulsive dieter who doesn't eat her dinner then raids the larder at night, gorging herself like there's no tomorrow . . . Rita Rudner plays this appalling woman, as if starring in her own TV show, where it's ten gags a minute. She can't blame the script because she co-wrote it. Even so, her performance clashes badly with her screen husband, Kenneth Branagh, who, apart from a dire drunk scene, turns in a winning performance. But since he also directed, I guess he's partly to blame for encouraging her. Back to our imaginary script conference.

'Now we need a part for Emma [Branagh's wife].'

'How about a nymphomaniac who only goes for married men? A real stunner.'

'Or we could go for something totally against type . . . make her a bit of a frump.'

'But full of good deeds.'

'Embarrasses everyone by giving Christmas presents even though it's New Year's Eve.'

'Good, good . . . wears smocks and eats brown rice. And secretly in love with Peter.'

'Gets desperate . . .'

'Bumps into him on the landing near midnight, drops her dressing gown . . .'

'Candlewick dressing gown and stands there starkers and says . . . and says:

"Fill me with your little babies."

'Great, great, then what does Peter do . . .'

'Same as any pouf. Run for his life, darling.' (*Laughter*)

'Great character, sort of modern Joyce Grenfell.'

'Er, yes, without the teeth – Emma's got perfect teeth.'

And so on.

In the event, Emma Thompson did play that role (a token black played the nymphomaniac). But even the actress of the year was unable to invest the character (who finally throws herself into the arms of Peter's chauffeur) with much credibility.

Best of this bunch of misfits is Imelda Staunton, as an anxious mother, always on the phone to the baby-sitter, to check on the health of her little boy whose twin suffered a tragic death – a device used as a running gag, at the mother's expense. Sounds like Rita Rudner again, as does the sentimental ending, when everyone stops bitching as they listen with growing horror to Peter's awful revelation. I wonder if their reactions would have been the same if his incurable disease had been a little less trendy – something like shingles or Alzheimer's. What we end up with is a small-scale TV sitcom made by the 'In' crowd.

The Crying Game, on the other hand, was wide screen, very wide appeal, cinematic, and, it must be said, very Hollywood. They loved it there. In fact they loved it all over the States.

A black man in blue jeans, arm around a sassy blonde, rolls drunkenly around a tatty Irish country fair, looking for a quiet place to fuck her. But he barely has time to get it out before he's jumped on by a bunch of boyos and bundled into a car. Gripping stuff. No parasols here, no good manners or emotions held in check. No mealy-mouthed small-minded stuff shot on 16 mill for the small screen. This is PANAVISION, shot by a director who knows his onions, knows the difference between film and tape, knows how to write a script that tells the story in pictures as well as words.

The kidnappers are members of the IRA. Their victim is a British soldier in mufti; the bait, blonde Miranda Richardson, in a mini-skirt. They hold the black soldier as hostage. He is kept under surveillance twenty-four hours a day and strikes up a relationship with one of the guards, played by Stephen Rea, who even holds his cock for him when he takes a pee. Whether he wipes his ass when he takes a shit we never know. That might be taking realism too far.

Negotiations with the Brits have reached stalemate. Time for the execution, with nice Stephen Rea delegated to pull the trigger and prove he isn't going soft. Will he, won't he; will he, won't he; will he pull the trigger? I am sitting on the edge of my seat. The condemned soldier is led into a wood by his executioner. Now the soldier is running away, with Rea racing after him, brandishing a gun and yelling blue murder. But both men are smiling, so it's going to be all right. The soldier turns briefly to wave goodbye as he runs into the road, straight under a truckload of squaddies come to rescue him. All hell breaks loose. Fire rains down from the sky, as helicopters turn the hideout into a blazing inferno. Wow! This is going to be one of the best British films for years, I think, diving into my bag of popcorn.

What next? The soft guard, whom we now recognise as the hero, decides to kill two birds with one stone by going to England – to pay his respects to the dead man's girlfriend, and to lie low from his mates in the IRA who might be wanting to ask him a question or two. Rea finds the girl and falls for her. The IRA find him, and say: Naughty boy, but we're going to give you another chance – to kill an old judge who goes to a certain brothel on a certain day at a certain hour every week. If you fail us this time, we'll kill your girlfriend and then kill you! 'Get it!' says Miranda Richardson in Cleopatra wig, high heels and Dior suit, as she grabs his balls and sticks a luger automatic up his nose.

But none of the goodies gets hurt, because this is a 'Made in America' movie where they only have happy endings. The IRA gang, or what's left of it, get their comeuppance, while the threatened lover blows Miranda away with her own shooter, thus saving the ex-IRA man's life. The last scene shows Rea being visited by his heroic lover in jail – implying that he will wait for him. Yes. The dead soldier's girlfriend was a man! A black man! Absolute twaddle.

Neil Jordan, who wrote and directed, is a good film maker. *Company of Wolves* and *High Spirits* had much to commend them. But with *The Crying Game* nonetheless, he has gone Hollywood (probably without even knowing it). He received an Oscar for Best Screenplay for his Troubles.

And what of BAFTA, Britain's answer to the Oscars? I suppose it's only a matter of time before we get the Sir Richard Attenborough Award, as he joins the roll call of our glorious dead whose names have been taken in vain to produce new 'Special Awards' –people like Michael Balcon, David Lean, Alexander Korda and Huw Wheldon. At this rate, the awards will soon outnumber the contestants and there will be prizes for everyone.

What, I wonder, happened to the Desmond Davies Award for an outstanding creative contribution to television, which I received in the late Sixties? Who *was* Desmond Davies, anyway? I doubt if any of 1993's back-slapping glitterati audience had ever heard of him.

The success of a film like *Howard's End* at the Oscars, BAFTA and elsewhere is depressing. Is this how the British cinema will end? Not with a bang, but a genteel whimper in full period costume. It is possible, as proved by the makers of *Leon the Pig Farmer*, to be original, inventive, contemporary and not spend more than £160,000. I made my film *Mahler* for the same amount, back in the early Seventies. Today *Mahler* couldn't be made for less than a million, which makes the achievement of Gary Sinyor and Vadim Jean miraculous. How did they do it? According to Sinyor, no one in the film was paid a penny, but everyone – crew and cast alike – agreed on a profit participation. The little money they raised was spent on production design, food, film and transport. And it looks as if everyone is set to be rewarded for the risk they took. And this will only serve to encourage others.

What is more, the film breaks new ground. Can you recall a single Jewish actor in any of those old Ealing comedies who portrayed anyone but a token Jew? This film redresses the balance. London bursts at the seams with Yiddish merrymaking. It seems you can't go into a single kosher gafilterbar without someone producing a fiddle and striking up a tune. Whereupon everyone leaps to their feet, forms a circle and joins in a Zorba the Greek-type dance that sets the joint jumping.

The story concerns a young Jewish boy who discovers that he owes his existence to a mix-up at an artificial insemination clinic. His real, biological father is not a Jewish lawyer but a Yorkshire pig farmer. What follows is a comedy of manners that also has a good deal to say about tolerance and identity. *Leon the Pig Farmer* exudes humour, warmth and humanity, qualities that Hollywood writers like Neil Simon are always trying to inject into their social comedies. But *Leon* beats Simon and his ilk because it is unforced and unconventional. I'm sure audiences in New York will love it, as they will in old York as well.

At last, a couple of Jewish film makers have come out of the closet, candelabras blazing, to proclaim their birthright, and to be a shining example to all of us who think we are hard done by, not only by the investors (or lack of them) but also by the government, which has gradually whittled away what few benefits and tax incentives the film industry ever had.

What of the British Film Establishment who take tea with the Prime Minister at Number Ten?

Well, there's a word for that lot, and we all know what it is. A French film maker told me the other day that, faced with a similar situation, he and his mates marched on Parliament, banners waving, and forced the President to listen to their demands. They hammered away until they got what they wanted.

Maybe we should do the same, chaps.

Any volunteers?

Index